Finding Home: from Leeds to London

an English girl's journey through foster care immediately after the Second World War.

Anna Berdahl

Printed in the United States of America
First Edition

To my children Sarah and Richard, who have brought such joy into my life,

and

In memory of Derman and Frances Christopherson, who offered me a permanent home and whose love and patience brought me the stability I so desperately needed.

Acknowledgements

There are many people who have encouraged me to write this memoir but very special thanks are due to the following friends: to Jill Pitkeathley and Julie Bayley, who read the first rough chapter and urged me to continue; to Virginia Thorndike and Irving Spitzberg, who enthusiastically supported me and offered their sage advice; to Denny Steinauer for scanning my photographs; to my editor Carol Andrews, who lovingly guided me through the daunting task and cured me of long paragraphs and dashes; and most of all to my dearest friend Rosalind, who since the age of eleven has been my constant support.

I also want to express gratitude to Vicky Grinrod of the West Yorkshire Archives and Jessica Talmage of the Mary Evans Picture Library for lending photographs for this memoir.

Contents

Preface

The initial goal in writing my story was to tell my children about the events and people that shaped me. I wanted them to recognize the limitations of my childhood and to forgive me for the mistakes I made in transferring some of these influences to their own upbringing. At the same time, I wanted them to know that other parts of my character made me a successful survivor and perhaps they could find a lesson in that.

I thought, too, that it would be interesting for them to understand what it was like growing up in a time they probably cannot imagine. Technology had not yet brought TV, let alone cell phones or the internet, to post war Britain, (even as late as 1970, my mother sent a congratulatory telegram when the twins were born rather than make a very expensive international phone call). Women did not wear trousers, literally or figuratively. Food was scarce and amusements, except for the cinema, were simple and mostly homemade.

Friends with whom I shared the initial draft of the first chapters felt strongly that the story had an audience beyond my children and so I expanded the narrative, always bearing in mind that this was not to be a fictional autobiography and I would not describe feelings or events that I do not remember experiencing in order to make the story more dramatic.

Finally, there were friends who were social workers and who were intensely interested not only in how foster care and adoptions were organized over seventy years ago, but who also wanted me to probe into why, after so many incidents of family loss and the critical absence of a father figure for the first fifteen years of my life, I had managed to turn out 'reasonably' (my word) well adjusted. To that I can only say that in many ways I was lucky both in the time I grew up and in the people I met at critical points in my life.

I was lucky because immediately after the war, communities, even in large cities, were close knit, pulling together to deal with the deprivations of rationing. Mothers stayed home and if you were up to mischief, they would hear about it from the neighbors.

I was lucky because violent crime, sexual abuse and alcoholism were never part of my life and it was safe for me to venture out by myself beyond my local streets, something that my grandchildren cannot do today. My upbringing, while it lacked affection, joy, and lightheartedness, also gave me a consistent core of morality taught to me by my foster parents and my schools. The variations of what was acceptable behavior and what was not as dictated by my different foster parents were more to do with class distinctions than basic right and wrong.

I was supremely lucky both because I had a brilliant primary school teacher who recognized I was bright and because my social worker, Miss Baker, left me temporarily with her neighbors, the Christophersons, when she went off for the Whitsuntide holidays.

As for my character, my sister said it was my imagination that carried me through, and others cited my optimistic personality. I leave my readers to decide for themselves.

I stood in angry silence, stubbornly refusing to look at my foster mother. I knew I was being difficult and moody but I had no idea how to find the words to connect with her. When I was upset, I simply shut down. No one had ever taught me to express my feelings or opinions, talk things over, consider both sides of an issue or defend myself. I couldn't risk opening up; I was too afraid of the consequences. At that moment I struggled with the terrible fear that things were going very wrong. Why was I behaving so badly? In my sixteen years of life I had been abandoned more than once and had faced frequent threats of being sent away if I did not behave. I was in a panic.

"Please break this impasse. I can't do it myself," I silently begged my foster mother.

Then she spoke.

She explained that she and her husband loved me very much. There would be more difficult times and their patience and my trust in them would be tested. But in the end, we would be joined as a family by the strongest threads which would never be broken. I was too overwhelmed to speak, but I knew in my heart that finally I had found home.

Chapter 1: 3, Wilson Court, Leeds
1943 – 1944
The First Memories

The disintegration of my birth family and the long journey to find a permanent and loving home began in my memory in a slum in the inner city of Leeds, a large industrial city in the north of England. I lived with my mother and four siblings in a terrace house on Wilson Court within walking distance of many members of my extended family, including three aunts and paternal grandparents.

The latter lived at 23, Renton Place, in one of the typical jerry-built, (flimsy) back-to-back terraces thrown up in haste by the industrial barons. They were built to accommodate thousands of mill and factory workers flocking in from the countryside in search of work. The houses covered the hillside in parallel rows with one outdoor toilet to every two families. I remember each household had a large iron key and had to take turns keeping the toilet clean. Newspapers and magazines hung on a nail served as toilet paper. Women hung their washing across the street, but not for long because soot from the coal fires and factory chimneys would quickly cover the clean clothes with a new grime.

Despite the dreariness of the terraces, the sameness of the houses, and the lack of flowers or anything green to soften their surroundings, the housewives took pride in the appearance of their small houses. They scrubbed the flagstones in front of their doors and scoured the edges of the window sills with a contrasting donkey stone.

A donkey stone was a product used to clean the greasy steps in the textile mills. The original company that made the stones had a donkey as its logo. Another source told me that the name came from the fact that the rag and bone men (junk collectors/ original recyclers) who toured the streets with their donkeys and carts, offered a free stone in return for castoff metal, clothes or anything else they could recycle.

Immaculate white lace curtains sparkled at the windows and woe to any woman who did not keep up these rigid standards and more. Years later, when my sister moved into a similar terrace house in her first year of marriage, she told me that she was visited by an old woman from across the street who warned her in no uncertain terms not to hang her washing out on a Sunday.

 "Good Christian families do not work on the Sabbath."

As a child I would see my grandparents' neighbors - mostly mothers and old men - sitting on their steps chatting to each other, but keeping an eye on all the children as we played. We had no toys but loved darting under the flapping washing held aloft by wooden props, and poking sticks on a hot day in the melting tar between the cobblestones.

Looming above the houses was the massive Armley Gaol, (pronounced Jail), a black castle-like structure built in 1847 and ever since a constant grim reminder to the locals to keep their noses clean. Years later, when all these terraces were razed and replaced with bright, modern little houses with small gardens, I was astonished to learn that in spite of the proximity of the Gaol, my aunts had happily moved back into this area.

In complete contrast, my own home was part of a row of four dismal houses and a butcher's shop reached by a narrow alley off the busy Wellington Road. Their doors faced inward to a rubbish filled yard occupied by rag and bone men and their carts, an outdoor toilet and pig sties. (Incongruous as it might seem, people in the inner city of Leeds had raised pigs for centuries to help supplement the family diet.) An embankment and railway line marked the furthest end of the yard.

This was a slum.

There was no neighborhood or community surrounding us and needless to say it cannot have been a safe environment to bring up children. Other than my mother, there was nobody to keep an eye on us.

Our house had one room on the ground floor and two small bedrooms upstairs. There was running water but no bathroom. The room downstairs was lit by gas and my mother cooked on a black-leaded range around the fireplace. There was a table in the center of the room and some chairs, and not much else.

Upstairs, one room held a bed and a small iron crib and the other room had a bed and some other furniture.

We were a family of six, seven if you count my father who was mostly away as a driver in the famous 8th Army. If his later boasting can be believed, he was part of the Allied Forces made up of British and Commonwealth troops. They defeated the great German Field Marshall Rommel, nicknamed the Desert Fox, in a crucial battle at El Alamein in North Africa. My only memory of him from these early years was when he came home on leave in time to celebrate my brother John's second birthday. The eldest child was Barry, just seven years old at the time of this narrative, then came me, Ann, aged four, Doris three, John two, and Norma one. We three girls were named after my father's sisters.

My mother, Doris Fox, called Dolly by most people, was sixteen when she lost her mother, then thirty-seven years old, to ovarian cancer. Her father worked in a copper factory and after his wife's death switched to the night shift so he could be there for the children during the day. Apparently, Dolly did not want to be responsible for caring for her younger siblings, Edna who was twelve and Freddy who was ten, so she soon married twenty-year-old John Spurr, an unemployed bricklayer with a hot temper who lived nearby. As soon as she was old enough, Edna joined the Forces and headed for London. It was rare for Yorkshire people to wander very far from where they were born, and Edna was one of the few family members to leave the county and settle in the "alien" South.

For a few years my mother was a caring parent, coping, at the age of twenty-four, with five children under eight years old. We lived in primitive conditions and most of the time she was without her husband. The only photograph I have of myself under the age of twelve shows me as a baby sitting on a chair and wearing a beautifully hand knitted outfit. Next to me stands Barry in a smart coat and with a neat haircut.

Clearly, at that time we were well dressed and cared for. I remember in the good times, for example, my mother ironing and placing neatly folded clothes around the fire to air. My mother was there when one day Barry chased me around the table, and I fell and hit my head on the sharp corner. I got up giggling until I felt something trickling down my face, saw the blood on my hand, and then screamed. My mother took me to the doctor's surgery, but it was closed for lunch, so we next tried the chemist. He treated my wound and bound up my head and I was thrilled with my bandage and no doubt the attention.

Then things changed, almost overnight.

My mother stopped caring for us, leaving us alone and hungry for hours. My Aunt Edna, whom I contacted years later, could not explain her drastic change in behavior. She had been away in the armed forces at the critical time and although she developed a close relationship with her sister in later years, she told me that my mother had never talked about the past. In the way of Yorkshire people, Aunt Edna would have never initiated such a conversation.

I have tried many times in my mind to understand and forgive her neglectful behavior. When my father was posted abroad in 1942, she chose to leave Catterick Garrison Camp, in North Yorkshire, where the family had been living and settled in Leeds because that put her a stone's throw away from where her in-laws and many of her relatives lived.

She was not without an adequate income because she received her husband's full army pay, which according to documents at the time was more than enough for her to manage the family budget.

On the other hand, there is no doubt that in addition to the struggle of raising her children alone and in such primitive circumstances, the deprivations and terror of war time must have made her life immensely challenging. She wrote later of the horror of going into labor with Norma as the bombs were falling. In addition, she was unhappily married. My father evidently had a violent streak and had once broken her father's nose in a quarrel. She also had ample proof that he was unfaithful to her.

For whatever the reasons, around June 1943, according to statements made at the time by my grandmother, my mother started to spend more and more of her time away from the home, taking a job as a cleaner on the railway, and consorting in the evenings with a bad crowd. She lost interest in her children, virtually abandoning us until a concerned neighbor and my grandmother stepped in.

During this time, Barry and I, as the two eldest, seemed to have had total freedom. We spent our time playing by the gasworks on the banks of the nearby Leeds and Liverpool Canal or climbing the embankment at the bottom of our yard to wander along the railway line where in summer rosebay willow herb and wild lupins grew. I followed him nervously as he explored the bombed house next to us. The dark and broken house terrified me, and I froze in terror at the sight of a scary iron crucifix on the wall, not knowing what it was. Even at times when my mother was at home during that year, it was amazing that we survived.

The scariest encounter, even though at the time I didn't recognize it, involved a tram. My mother used to send me on errands across Wellington Road, a major road heading west out of central Leeds, to the Maypole, a small grocery store. On one such trip, something caught my eye as I crossed the street and I simply sat down to examine it. A tram came to a clanging halt inches from me, and the driver yelled angrily at me to get out of the way. I ambled across the road wondering what all the fuss was about.

Barry must have been in school a good deal of the time, so as the next oldest I was often the one in charge. I remember it was my job to make sure the gate was across the doorway, so my baby sister Norma could not crawl into the yard. I don't remember Norma ever being taken out in a pushchair, so it is quite possible she never left the house. Sometimes John and I were given money to go to the cinema. We were far too young to be allowed to enter unaccompanied, so we would ask older people (probably teenagers) to buy the tickets for us and then we slipped in.

At some stage I became aware of how much our lives had changed for the worse, brought on by the neglect and frequent absences of our mother. Barry taught me how to slice bread, which often seemed to be the only thing we could find to eat, and I would sometimes accompany my grandmother down the hill from her house as she brought us plates of food.

Desperately hungry, I watched a little girl eating an apple in the window of a nearby house and begged her for the peel. I asked her if I could come inside and play, but she said her mother had told her I was too dirty to be allowed in her house.

Things came to a head when a neighbor, who had been urging my grandmother for weeks to contact the Authorities, sent an anonymous letter to the National Society for the Prevention of Cruelty to Children (N.S.P.C.C.), complaining of our appalling living conditions and reporting that my mother frequently left us unsupervised all night to go off dancing in the nearby pub, the Star and Garter.

My grandmother was told about the intervention of the neighbor and came immediately and found some food for us.

The Society responded by sending an officer immediately to investigate. After taking note of the downstairs which was incredibly filthy, he went upstairs, and I trailed behind him, fearful at what I knew he would surely find. He entered the small bedroom where four of us slept on a filthy mattress covered by dirty army blankets, and I remember vividly my acute embarrassment when he flung back the blankets and saw the feces and urine stains mixed in with stale pieces of jam and bread. The officer left to give his report and then my mother turned up to face an angry mother-in-law. She defended herself by saying she had only left us briefly while she went to buy food, but in reality, she had been celebrating the New Year all night and hadn't bothered to wait to make sure the girl she supposedly asked to mind us had turned up.

According to official reports, the officer returned at 2:15 with an Assistant Director and a police surgeon and the decision was made that for the sake of our health and safety we should be removed from my mother's care. An ambulance arrived, and as I climbed into it, I passed my mother, a petite woman with long dark hair, who was sobbing inconsolably. Frightened by this, I started crying too until a kind nurse consoled me with a coin.

According to other reports I later read, John, Norma and I were taken to St. James Hospital, where we stayed for sixteen days. We were suffering from septic sores and in addition Norma had a severe ear infection. Barry and Doris were sent directly to Street Lane Home, where we joined them on January 21, one day before my fifth birthday. The only memory I have of the Home at this time was a visit by my grandparents. Alas, I had developed chicken pox and could only wave at them from the window.

On February 2, my mother appeared before a magistrate and was prosecuted for willful neglect. She was ordered to pay a fine of just over £6, about the same amount that she earned per week. In addition, both parents had to pay child support to the local authorities for Mary, John and me. A hearing in Juvenile Court to determine what should happen to us was scheduled in April, but the NSPCC had trouble finding her to serve her with a notice to appear. It is not clear whether she did, in fact, attend the hearing in that court, which was held in early May.

My father was granted compassionate leave and his petition to take custody of Barry was approved, awarding my brother to his paternal grandparents for temporary care. Norma was adopted by a local family and I never saw either one of them again. Another family stepped forward to adopt Doris and me. Apparently during the time my mother was still functioning as a caring parent, they remembered us as two cute little girls with bright blond hair in matching pigtails (I was nicknamed Snowball) but their request was denied. I think it happened because the father was a soldier and was away most of time. So, the three of us were "boarded out" as it was called, i.e., placed in foster homes.

My father obtained a divorce and eventually remarried. My mother also remarried and had six more children, all boys. Her husband was petrified by my father's bad temper and ordered her not to have contact with anyone from her previous marriage, including her children.

I never saw or heard from my parents again until my father appeared out of the blue when I was fourteen, and I tracked down my mother when I was an adult.

P Y.

Sir,

I am writing you hoping as soon as ever you can to get in touch with Mrs. Spurr of Wilson Court off Wellington Road Leeds 12 concerning her family of five children Her Husband is Serving Abroad The Eldest child Age 7 was once a bright boy but I am afraid with her sheer neglect is going to a little Wreck. The youngest child Norma 18 months as never to my knowledge been out of Doors and is positively full off Rickets The House is Dirty The children are always left to themselves and at night she goes dancing and Drinking in Leeds Brooms Arms and the Star and Garter Kirstall in fact Christmas Eve she never came home while eleven o'clock next morning the children where laid in Chairs all night alone with a Candle Burning on the Shelf and now to Crown all matters she has taken a job on the Railway and leaves them to a Girl to mind. She has a good Army Pay and what I write is Perfectly true. If you want any more information Please call at her Mother-in-laws 23 Renton Place, Leeds. 12 who knows all about her but was so long in letting you know I have beat her to it for the Kiddies Sake

(Signed) Lover of children

Anonymous letter from a concerned neighbor

Police Surgeon's Rooms,
Town Hall,
LEEDS.1.

5th January,1944.

Sir,

re:- The Spurr Family at 3,Wilson Court.

At 2.15 p.m. on the above date I examined the premises and three members of the family of Mrs.Spurr who was then present. The remaining children were out and could not be found.

The house consisted of a living room, two bedrooms and a coal cellar. The living room had an adequate amount of furniture but was indescribably filthy. The first bedroom had in it a double bed on which was an old mattress and a bolster without cover, three army blankets and an army greatcoat. The whole of these articles were saturated with recent and ammoniacal urine and in the folds was recent and old excreta mixed indiscriminately with pieces of bread and jam and filth of all descriptions. There was also a child's cot which was devoid of bedding. The room itself was filthy, there were no other articles of furniture, no floor coverings and the whole place was littered with debris.

The back bedroom contained an old single bedstead dismantled and an old wringer. On the floor was a miscellaneous collection of foul clothing. Another bundle of foul clothing was found on the stairs.

The family consisted of the father who was in the Army, the mother who is employed on the railway and the following children, Barrie aged 7, Ann aged 5, Doris aged 4, John aged 2½, and Norma aged 1½. John, who was in a filthy condition, his lower limbs being covered with sores, was running around the kitchen entirely naked with the exception of a small tattered pullover. Norma was clothed in a woolly dress and cotton vest and had on a pair of shoes. She was suffering from otitis media and had septic sores on the lower limbs. Doris had on a dress and coat and sandshoes.

The children did not show any signs of malnutrition, and with the exception of Doris, who was brought round for examination from her auntie's, they were extremely filthy and inadequately clothed.

The only food in the house appeared to be two parts of a loaf of bread which had been got out for the children's dinner. The larger piece which was almost a complete loaf, had been partly consumed by mice. The second piece, about a 1/6 part of a loaf, appeared wholesome but very dry.

The Army Allowance received by this woman is £3.12.6d. plus a 7/- grant per week. Her own wage from the railway, a position she has only held for a short time, is £2. 4. 0d. a week. Her rent is 7/- a week.

In my opinion, these children should be removed and the conditions under which they are living and particularly the state of health of two of them is likely to cause unnecessary suffering and permanent injury to their health.

(Signed) Hoyland Smith.

Police Surgeon's Report

24

Boarding out (Placement) records for the Spurr children

Credit: The Yorkshire Evening Post February 2, 1944

My maternal great grandmother's family, the Duftons: From left to right in the back: Florrie, Ivy, Lizzie, great granddad, Edith (my grandmother); seated in front, great grandmother with cousin Ivy.

My maternal grandparents, Fred and EdithFox.

My mom, Doris Fox, age 16

Aunt Edna and Uncle Ted
during World War II

Uncle Freddy

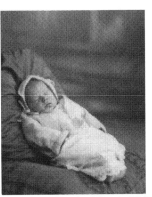

My brother Barry and me, 1939

My sister Doris (Mary), 1940

3, Wilson Court (third house from the right), demolished in the 60's and replaced with a petrol station.

Reference: WYAS, LC/ENG/Clearance, Radnor Street (Wellington Road) Box 94/7

My mother and her second husband, Patrick Douglas

Central (Street Lane) Home
Credit: Peter Higginbotham Collection/Mary Evans

Chapter 2: Poole Crescent, Leeds
1944-1947
5-8 years old

Given that there surely must have been a large number of orphans and displaced people as the war ground on, it is amazing that a foster home was found for me in just over three months after my arrival at Street Lane Home. Now, completely severed from my entire family, I arrived at my new home at Poole Crescent to my foster mother, Mrs. Thomas, with a few possessions and my ration book provided by some mysterious persons called the Local Authorities.

Poole Crescent was part of a group of council houses (public housing) in Cross Gates in the eastern part of Leeds and a long way from where I had previously lived. The house, modest though it was, must have seemed like a palace to me. It was certainly a great improvement on the slum that I had left behind. It had a living room and kitchen downstairs, and two bedrooms and a real bathroom upstairs, with a small garden in front and a garden with an air raid shelter at the back. There must not have been any trees along the street as I recall Mrs. Thomas telling me that a neighbor moved from her house to one nearby simply because from the new house she could see some bushes and trees in the gap between the houses opposite. Later in America, I noticed how much trees softened the ugliness of poor neighborhoods and understood this woman's need for the sight of greenery.

Mrs. Thomas was a war widow and I remember seeing a picture of her husband in uniform in the living room. I do not know when he died, but I always thought of her as an old lady, although a five-year-old's perception of what is old is not reliable. She was foster mother to two other girls, one called Shirley, who was quite a bit older than I, and another whom I never met because she was in a remand home for climbing out of the bedroom window at night and running off with boys.

Mrs. Thomas was a very kind person and did a great deal to stabilize me. She understood the importance of consistency and order in a child's life, particularly for one who had lived in unsupervised chaos for so long. The meals and bedtime were at regular times, and we look forward to listening to a program called "Dick Barton, Special Agent" on the radio. One night after we had gone to bed, there was a very noisy thunderstorm, and although I don't remember being afraid, Mrs. Thomas thought that we should come downstairs until the storm had passed and we had the special treat of listening to the Sunday night concert of the Palm Court Orchestra.

Every night, Mrs. Thomas would see us into bed, turn out the light, and when she was at the bottom of the stairs I would call out "Bread and dripping for breakfast?" and she would always answer yes. (Every English housewife kept a basin of beef dripping which was used for frying. Dripping was also spread on bread or toast and sprinkled with salt. Delicious brown beef jelly collected at the bottom of the basin and it was a very lucky person who was allowed to spread that on toast. I shudder at the cholesterol levels of this diet. On the other hand, with severe rationing continuing well after the war, this was probably as good a source of fat as any to help people survive.)

Although I had lost my whole family and for reasons that I only vaguely understood, I find it puzzling that I have no memory of crying for my mother or asking about my brothers and sisters or behaving in ways that are common in children who have suffered the traumas of family separation. Perhaps the months of decline of my comparatively secure life with my mother had already prepared me a little for the loss to come, but I should have mourned particularly for Barry, who had been my constant companion and lifeline during that difficult time.

The easy answer that therapists would offer was that I buried the hurt and confusion of those grim memories in order to survive. Clearly, the pain of abandonment and loss was deep in my bones and that pain reappeared often through my life, no more piercingly than when my own children and grandchildren reached the age of five. It was inconceivable to me that these beloved children would have thrived as I eventually did after such a devastating loss.

Nevertheless, in my new life, I seem to have been a relatively happy and resilient child, eager to embrace all the new experiences being offered to me. I had no toys so I played with what was around me. The wonderful seeds of hollyhocks became pretend food for my tea parties. I gathered the petals from roses and added them to water in a jam jar to make perfume until Mrs. Thomas threw it away in the dustbin, disgusted no doubt by the rotten smell.

School was another reason that I thrived. I attended Cross Gates Primary, an easy walk from my home. When I arrived at my foster home, my vocabulary was limited (I remember being offered a tart and not knowing what that was), but once at school, I devoured everything the teacher fed me and was soon reading well. I remember being paraded in different classrooms to demonstrate how good a reader I was at such an early age. No doubt the older kids who were struggling with reading must have hated me!

It was during my time with Mrs. Thomas that I became slowly aware that I was different from other children. For one thing, I had to call my foster mother Aunty, a practice presumably recommended by the foster care system. This was to become an enormous source of embarrassment and anguish for me in later years as I struggled to avoid the necessity of explaining the discrepancy between my last name and that of my foster family. Divorce in England was rare at that time and even though there must have been war orphans, I knew of no one else in my situation. My brother John writes movingly of the anguish he felt at not having the same name as his parents.

In a poor neighborhood, we were even poorer. Mrs. Thomas supplemented her income by cleaning the house of a woman who lived across Cross Gates Road, a natural divider of the council estate where we lived on the one side and the more affluent semi-detached houses on the other. Sometimes she was given eggs or flowers by the woman, and she complained that she would have preferred extra cash.

An incident on a flag day at school illustrated how poor she was and also became my first lesson in honesty. In those days and even now, English charities raised money by having volunteers stand on street corners and offer a small paper flag with a pin to put on the lapel in exchange for a donation. By wearing the flag, you showed that you had donated and you would not be stopped again. The flags at school were for sale for a penny, but Mrs. Thomas said she couldn't afford that. I was immensely disappointed not to be like my other classmates, but then I found a flag on the playground and pinned it proudly on my jersey. I noticed it had someone's name on the back, but I chose to ignore that. Mrs. Thomas immediately discovered the name and demanded I take it back to school, chiding me gently for my dishonesty. This incident made a profound impression on me and one later occurrence of dishonesty that I can remember kept me in an agony of guilt for weeks. For years, I was always hungry and once when waiting in a shop to buy some sweets, I couldn't resist helping myself to a small dog biscuit that was sitting there temptingly in a big open sack. It did not taste good so there was no chance I would do that again.

Although we were poor and I noticed the small differences between other families and me, I never felt deprived. I attended school, had girlfriends to play with, ate sparse but regular meals and did not lack for decent clothes. I did not yearn for a better life because I had no idea what that would look like.

The war does not seem to have been a frightening experience for me. Air raid shelters by this time were just damp places to play in, gas masks shaped like Mickey Mouse were objects of curiosity, ration cards and clothing coupons were more the concern of my foster mother, and I certainly would not have understood the significance of the heavy crisscross taping across the windows of my primary school. I have no memory of the much-documented joyous street parties celebrating the end of the war, but I do remember coming home from school with special treasures to commemorate the victory. Each child received a special mug and a "parchment" letter from His Majesty George VI, presumably declaring the end of the war and commending the British people for their valor and sacrifices.

My experience of the world at this time was for the most part limited to the street where I lived, the school I attended, and a short walk to the local shops or the library, although I do remember going with Shirley for a walk in a wood to gather bluebells. It turned into a frightening experience.

We had gone well into the wood when we heard the sound of teenagers laughing and talking. Suddenly, two boys came crashing through the trees and stopped us. One of them tackled Shirley and tried to get her knickers off as she screamed and thrashed around. The other boy, who was clearly uncomfortable with the whole thing, picked up Shirley's flowers which she had dropped on the ground and gave them to me to hold. I did not know what to do but kept on saying "Aunty is coming any minute." Eventually, the boy gave up and the two left. Shirley chided me angrily for not helping her but I didn't know what to do and I wasn't even sure what was going on. I don't believe Shirley told our aunty what had happened and certainly no police were involved.

Years later, I watched the film Blow Up (1966) in which there was a scene involving the two main characters who thrashed around on the floor in a fairly violent but consensual sexual encounter. The loud crackling of the paper or clothing they were lying on brought back a terrifying flashback of the incident with Shirley, and I had to close my eyes and grip my seat until the scene was over.

Only once did we venture outside of Leeds, let alone Cross Gates, and it was not a happy experience. Mrs. Thomas decided that we would travel to York to see a relative and we set off on a dreary, damp day for the station in the center of Leeds. On arriving at York, we had a long walk to the house where this relative lived. As we approached, Mrs. Thomas noticed the gasman going into the garden of the relative's house and then reappearing immediately. She groaned because she knew that he would not have had time to enter the house to empty the meter and therefore no one was home. She chided herself for not having written ahead of time, (nobody that I knew in those days owned a phone), but there was nothing for us to do but start the long walk back to the station. It obviously did not occur to her that there might have been interesting things for children to see in York. Visiting friends or relatives was the only "special" activity that mattered in her narrow world. So we trailed back to the station and sat on the platform eating some sandwiches while we waited miserably for the train home. Mrs. Thomas must have deeply regretted spending precious money for this abortive trip.

Sometime during my eighth year, my stable world was rocked again when I was informed by the boarding out officer that Mrs. Thomas was ill, and we were going to stay with another "Aunty" until she got better. I remember that Mrs. Thomas couldn't swallow certain things such as bacon and I have often wondered if in fact, she had throat cancer. Of course, we were never told. Shirley and I were taken to a Mrs. Walker, who lived on the same street as the woman for whom Mrs. Thomas cleaned.

We never saw Mrs. Thomas again and I assume she died.

No explanations were given, no chance to grieve, and once again I had to deal with loss and disruption, and this time secrecy. I lived in a world that still believed in children being seen and not heard, and the idea that they needed to be counseled and helped to prepare them for another traumatic separation was not part of the thinking.

Chapter 3: 17, Hawkhill Drive, Leeds
1947-1951
8-12 years old

Mr. and Mrs. Walker had two boys, Norman and Cyril, who had grown up and married and had children of their own. Cyril had a young daughter, Carol, and had some kind of job that involved driving a van. He lived in Wakefield, an area which I associated with endless fields of cabbages. Norman was the quiet musical son who worked for an organ building company on Hough Lane in Armley. He had a son called Peter, the apple of his grandparents' eye, and later girl twins, one of whom died.

After the war, married women, who had worked in the munitions factories or on farms, resumed the role of full-time housewives. The men had returned to claim their former jobs and I imagine that Mrs. Walker, even with grandchildren, was lonely and bored alone in the house all day. Severe rationing made cooking a constant struggle and there was little petrol for trips for those lucky enough to have some form of transport.

She did not seem to have close friends, and there was no parade of neighbors popping in for a chat, so perhaps taking in foster children was a way of relieving her boredom. She may well have had altruistic reasons or perhaps she wanted the experience of bringing up a girl. It was a long time before I began to give some real thought as to why people were interested in becoming foster parents. Initially, I assumed that it was because they wanted someone to love, and I was that someone. Such expectations were common among foster children and almost always doomed them to disappointment and sometimes anger. Much later, I came to realize that there was a financial incentive to fostering children.

The Walkers' house was much superior to those of the council houses of Poole Crescent, and once again I had moved up a notch on the rigid class system. Not only was there a small kitchen and living room, but a front room or lounge where all the best furniture was kept. The bay window of this room faced the street and treasured knickknacks were placed along the broad window sill to be admired both by those inside and those passing by.

I hated this cold, sterile room, although it was obviously the pride and joy of my foster parents.

The furniture consisted mostly of a three-piece suite, a sofa and two matching armchairs covered in transparent plastic when not in use, and floor lamps with tasseled shades. The house boasted a front door, but just like the lounge, it was rarely used. A knock at that door almost always meant that someone was asking to use the telephone since neighbors who occasionally came to borrow a bit of sugar or the like always used the back or side door and they were never invited in. The Walkers were one of the few people in the neighborhood to own a phone andthose who needed to use it brought money to pay for the call. A call made at a public phone cost four pennies, which were large copper coins the size of silver dollars. I cannot imagine how people such as reporters managed to carry all those heavy coins in their pockets so they could make their many important calls. Local calls were charged by time just as long distance calls were, so you had to talk quickly before a series of warning pips sounded and you were requested to add more money. I was in awe of the telephone because of the status it obviously gave to my foster parents and because I was strictly forbidden to touch it. It was years later before I could overcome my inhibitions and stop asking permission to use the phone. To this day, although I enjoy chatting on the phone with friends and family, I absolutely loathe initiating calls and when I arrive home after an outing, I am always relieved when the answering machine shows nobody left a message.

Upstairs was a bathroom, a separate toilet, and three bedrooms. The Walkers had the largest bedroom, Shirley and I were given the other large room, and there was a very small bedroom often called a box room where people traditionally stored suitcases and other things.

Shirley and I surveyed our new room with wonderment. We had never seen such a fancy room, with its large double bed and mirrored dressing table on which lay an exciting array of treasures, a matching set of brushes, combs and hand mirror, and beautiful glass perfume bottles. We bounced on the bed with joy, brushed our hair and primped in the mirror, and sprayed ourselves with perfume, much to the horror of our new Aunty, who removed everything from the dressing table and admonished us severely for our wild behavior.

While living with Mrs. Thomas, I had learned to keep my place as the younger girl and deferred to Shirley in most things. But once at the Walkers things changed. Perhaps because I had gained self-confidence from my successes at school, or perhaps at age eight one tends to become more assertive, but most likely I was fiercely defending my turf, determined not to share any meager signs of affection that might come my way from the Walkers, I began to fight with Shirley. In the end, Mrs. Walker must have grown tired of dealing with our squabbles and Shirley was sent to another foster home.

"I hope you're satisfied" was her parting shot.

Later, my sister Doris, who was now called Mary, an arbitrary decision made by one of her foster parents, came to share this home for a brief time but I drove her away too. I remember to my shame throwing a hairbrush at her and yelling "Good riddance to bad rubbish" as she fled down the street. My sister laughs when we recall this memory, recognizing it as sibling rivalry but with a great deal more at stake.

In the first year or so, daily life with the Walkers was very predictable. Food was still in short supply after the war and nearly all basic foods were severely rationed. Occasionally, items such as tinned peaches or guavas were available and people hoarded them for special occasions such as a 25th wedding anniversary.

There was much gossip and resentment about certain people in the neighborhood, especially the butcher, who was rumored to have dealt on the black market.

Since supermarkets did not exist at this time in Britain, much of the housewife's time was spent in queuing at different shops. I remember the long lines at the fish shop and the use of BU's (bread units) to purchase bread. The meager meat rations were supplemented by Spam, imported from the USA, and tinned corned beef. Sandwich fillings were usually something in little jars called potted meat or fish paste, and failing all else potato crisps or even steak sauce.

Certain parts of the population such as pregnant women and young children were given extra rations. I remember some children who were presumably designated as malnourished or at risk, lining up in the classroom every day and being given a big dollop of malt and cod liver oil by the teacher. I did not qualify for this treat, but I tried it once and it was delicious as the sweet sticky malt masked the nasty taste of cod liver oil.

Nurses and dentists also visited the schools. We queued up to receive shots or vaccinations and I was proud that I didn't cry. At the age of nine I was given a plate by the school dentist to straighten my top teeth but no follow up took place, so my bottom teeth remained forever crooked and crowded. Later, all children in school received every day one-third of a pint of milk which was delivered in bottles.

Clothing was also rationed, presenting an enormous challenge to the housewife. Every scrap of material was saved. Clothes were patched, hems let down, jerseys unraveled and the wool reused. I remember my foster mother dyeing her white blouse navy as it made her feel that she had a brand-new garment. Some people were lucky enough to get hold of damaged parachute silk and used it to make dresses for weddings or other special occasions.

Some of the clothing allowance had to be set aside for blackout curtains. Old men and others who were exempt from service became wardens, whose job it was to patrol the neighborhood looking for any chink of light that might guide enemy aircraft to their target.

At the Walkers, breakfast in the winter was a bowl of porridge sweetened by Tate & Lyle Golden Syrup and in summer there was the inevitable single slice of bread and dripping sprinkled with salt. Some kind of meat, usually mutton or tripe if available, was produced for Sunday dinner. (Dinner in Yorkshire refers to the lunchtime meal, whereas the evening meal was called tea). Once I refused to eat the grisly meat, hungry as I was, when I learned it was sheep's head, so of course I had to make do with potatoes and whatever vegetable was offered, usually cabbage, swedes, turnips or brussel sprouts. Pudding, if there was any, was usually stewed rhubarb. Like the cabbages, rhubarb flourished in Leeds. I remember the huge thick stalks of this pink plant growing in everyone's garden.

Monday was the day I hated most, especially in the winter. Every British housewife did her washing on that day. It was a day long affair starting with hauling up a zinc tub from the cellar, filling it with hot water, scrubbing the clothes and sheets on a washboard, rinsing them, rolling them through the mangle to get rid of excess water and then hanging them out on the line across the street or in the back garden. Once partially dry, the clothes and linens were ironed and then placed on a clothes horse around the coal fire, filling the room with steam and cutting off the only source of heat in the house.

Monday's dinner was predictable: leftover cold meat from Sunday, boiled potatoes and pickled beets. Occasionally I was allowed to go to the fish and chip shop and ask for a pennyworth of scraps (left over bits of fried batter from the fish) or given a few lemonade crystals or cocoa and sugar in place of sweets, which were rationed.

I had a small weekly allowance which I spent at the local sweet shop and once there took forever to make my choice from the tantalizing array of tall jars full of wonderful concoctions. Boiled sweets such as pear drops and anything made of liquorice were my favorite but on the other hand aniseed balls or gob stoppers lasted longer. I also enjoyed sweet cigarettes. They were sticks of sugar with red tips and packaged to look very like the real thing, not something that could even be imagined today, but we enjoyed pretending to smoke them as we imitated the grownups.

England is a nation of sweet eaters and I remember the enormous excitement when sweets were finally derationed in April 1949. We queued up at the little shop next to the cinema to load up on the yearned for treats. However, the demand was so huge that the beleaguered shopkeeper had finally to limit everyone to just a quarter of a pound! By August of that same year, sweets were back on ration and remained so until 1953, the year of the Queen's Coronation.

I was always hungry and found a way of supplementing my diet by sheer force of my personality. I started a club at playtime in which everyone shared the snack they had brought from home, except I never had a snack. For some reason they accepted this as the price of being in my club. Once when I was taken to the doctor to have a festering splinter removed from my hand, Mrs. Walker asked why I was so thin. He replied that children were like horses: some were heavy plodders like the big shire horses, and others were lean race horses, and clearly I was a race horse. I remember vividly the absolute rage and frustration I felt at this answer since it was clear to me that a little more to eat would have solved the problem and I would have happily turned into a shire horse!

Mrs. Walker had strange rules. For example, I was never allowed to go into her bedroom, not even to glance inside. After school and on the weekends, I was expected to play out in all weathers and was forbidden to go into the homes of any of my friends. Perhaps this was to protect me, although she must have known all the neighbors and people were much more trusting in those days. Perhaps she did not want to be put in the position of having to reciprocate. I certainly was never allowed to invite anybody into the house, even on a rainy day.

I had very few toys except a skipping rope and a ball and so spent hours perfecting my skills with both. I taught myself to ride a bike by borrowing a full-sized one from a friend. Children in England in those days did not have play clothes so inevitably when I fell off the big bike as I learned to ride it; I tore my dress and got into a lot of trouble. Metal roller skates were fun and because they could be adjusted to foot size with the use of a key, I could borrow these too from my friends. I skated along the parade in front of the cinema and practiced various daring moves such as the "flying swan". When the weather was too bad for me to play outside, I read my library books, or did jigsaws which I was passionately fond of and still am to this day.

Since I couldn't be left outside in the winter when the Walkers made their weekly trip to the cinema, I was taken along. *The Red Shoes*, a film starring Moira Shearer about ballet dancing enthralled me and was the reason I have had a lifelong passion for ballet. I spent hours outside, leaping, pirouetting, and toe pointing, trying to emulate the dancers I had seen on the screen. I quickly wore out my cheap rubber shoes (forerunner of sneakers) called plimsolls, much to the annoyance of my foster mother.

There were some bright spots in this dull and predictable life. Many religious holidays were celebrated such as Shrove Tuesday, called Pancake Day by the children. Mothers made crepes, tossing each one in the air and catching them in the pan before filling with jam.

In Yorkshire at Whitsuntide, White Sunday, celebrated in the Christian church to commemorate the descent of the Holy Spirit on the Apostles, children were given new clothes (not me of course) and went around the neighborhood to show them off. We were also given whips and tops. The tops were round and squat and the whip was a leather strip attached to a stick. Children decorated the tops with colored chalk so when the tops spun, they made beautiful patterns. I had a top of my own but no chalks, so I used the ones at the blackboard at school to decorate its face. My goal was to whip my top all the way to school, keeping it spinning until it was safe to cross busy Cross Gates Road and the tramlines in the middle, no easy feat. A new top appeared that was all the rage. It was super thin and when whipped correctly, could be made to jump a long way. Broken windows were the result of these leaping tops and so were banned by many parents, but I didn't care because I much preferred my solid old top.

For a brief time, I belonged to the Brownies at St. James church and went with them on a picnic at Whitsuntide. Regardless of the chilly weather, the girls wore their summer dresses (with the inevitable cardigan) and sandals. We rode to a local farm in the back of a lorry, screaming with joy as the breeze blew our hair, intrigued by a maypole in one of the villages we drove through. We had a lot of fun running races and playing games, although getting our sandals covered in cow clap was not so enjoyable! Whitsuntide is a name now barely recognizable in a mostly secular country and instead the three-day holiday at the end of May is called by the dull name of Bank Holiday.

Another celebration beloved by children was Bonfire Night, or Guy Fawkes Night as it is sometimes called, which takes place each year on November 5th. It commemorates the foiling of the Gunpowder Plot in 1605, when a man called Guy Fawkes was arrested as he guarded explosives under the House of Lords. He was part of a plot by a group of Catholics to blow up Parliament during the time when the Protestant King James I was present. The nation celebrated the arrest with bonfires and fireworks and effigies of Fawkes were burned.

In Yorkshire, the day before Bonfire Night is called Mischief Night, when children play tricks on people. Mostly, it involves the annoying but harmless act of ringing the neighbors' doorbells and running away, but for some it was an excuse for vandalism and many a garden gate was removed and added to the bonfire.

As children, we spent weeks collecting wood and other things to burn (in Yorkshire this is called "chumping"), and we made a stuffed man, the "Guy" who would be burned on the fire. Some children would often take the Guy in a homemade cart or a pushchair to busy corners of the street, outside pubs, or bus and railway stations and plead for "a penny for the Guy". The money collected was spent on fireworks.

It was a glorious time. Fathers would set up the fireworks and we watched rockets go shooting into the air, and the Catherine Wheels and Roman Candles showering us with colorful sparks. We screamed with both horror and delight as the boys threw jumping crackers at our feet.

In Yorkshire, mothers made parkin, a kind of local gingerbread, and treacle toffee, and carefully placed large potatoes in the hot ashes. We poked them with our sticks and eventually were allowed to take them out and eat them. Nothing tasted as wonderful as those barely cooked potatoes with their blackened skins.

Sadly nowadays in Britain bonfires and fireworks are not allowed for safety reasons unless organized by the local municipality. I am told that Halloween is gradually replacing Bonfire Night, which is funny when you realize that Halloween originated in Ireland, was introduced into America, and is now returning to Britain.

Christmas was not much of a celebration in the years immediately following the war, although we had a party at school with sandwiches, jellies and iced buns as a special treat. We decorated the classroom and we made Christmas cards to take home. I have no memory of looking forward with eager anticipation to Christmas, although I imagine I was given a few presents – perhaps the jigsaws I loved so much and my first doll at age eight.

My foster parents made very little effort to introduce religion to me, although on a whim they sometimes sent me to Sunday school and on a rare occasion, took me to a service. While I washed the dishes after Sunday dinner, they read *The News of the World*, a ghastly tabloid which I was forbidden to read. Of course, I would snatch a glance at it from time to time and it seemed to be full of stories about people who were "intimate" in the back seat of cars. I had no idea what that meant but I deduced it was something bad!

They also did the Pools (betting on football games) and I gathered that correctly forecasting the draws seemed to be the way to great riches, although I do not think the Walkers won much money, if any. I vividly remember listening to the announcer on the radio reading out the results. Oh the magical names of those teams: Wolverhampton Wanderers, Tottenham Hotspurs, and Scottish Midlothian!

My foster father was my first experience of having a permanent male in the household, but he was a shadowy figure and played no active role in my upbringing. He got up early and went to work, returned by six for his tea and then disappeared in the garden to dig or lost himself in the *Yorkshire Evening Post*. One day I was told to go talk to him in the garden as he had a surprise for me. He announced that we were going to the seaside for the day. No community in England is further than seventy-five miles from the sea and yet of course I had never seen it. I wasn't sure what it all meant but there was a flurry of activity in preparation for this trip, including the arrival of the daughters-in-law, who began to frantically knit me a bathing suit. I was allowed to stay up late and given the task of knitting the straps while enjoying the chit chat of the women and eating the snacks they prepared. Getting extra food was always a big deal for me.

We left for Scarborough, a seaside town on the north-east coast, in a van provided by Cyril. It must have been an exciting occasion for my foster parents who never seemed to go anywhere, but I was not impressed by the sea or the trip. It was a chilly day, the water was grey and oppressive, and I had no idea what to do with the bucket and spade I had been given. On the way back, we stopped at a pub. In those days, children were not allowed to enter pubs so I was left alone in the van with a packet of crisps and a Tizer - a popular fizzy drink known for its slogan "Tizer the Appetizer". Nowadays my foster parents would probably have been arrested for leaving a small girl in a van alone in a dark parking lot while they drank in the pub, but that was quite common in those days.

As the income of the Walkers improved, we took an annual holiday of a whole week at the seaside, Scarborough, Bridlington, and Filey on the Yorkshire north-east coast being the most popular destinations. At first, the Walkers shared a hired caravan with some of their family but when the economy improved again, they moved up to a boarding house. These establishments were often run by widows and were usually three story terrace houses. They had names often evoking exotic places in the world, perhaps a reference to some past travel by the owner, or a way of attracting the attention of sentimental tourists. Sea View was a common name, although often the only view of the sea was from the top floor of the house. We were served breakfast and dinner in the dining room, all eaten for the most part in polite silence except for occasional comments on the weather. The smell of cabbage pervaded the whole house. Guests were not encouraged to linger in the house during the day.

This habit of not chatting casually to people one didn't know stemmed I think from a very English attitude that to do so would be intrusive. I was once traveling by train from Durham to London in an old-fashioned compartment where you sat facing people in close proximity and we all either retreated behind our newspapers, read our books, or gazed out of the window, and not a word was spoken for most of the journey. Just outside Kings Cross Station in London the train was held up in a tunnel for a considerable time. After ten minutes, a man got up and peered into the dark and made some comment and it was as though a dam had broken or an internal signal switched on giving us permission to talk. We all immediately began to relate stories of similar railway problems and by the time the train resumed its slow entry into the station, we had exchanged personal details as though we were long lost friends.

This love of naming one's house is very common in England. While it is understandable that this should be so in the country where the villages had few streets and where it seemed appropriate to call one's house Mill Cottage if it was indeed (or used to be) situated by a mill, or Laburnum Tree House even if there is no longer such a tree in the front garden, in the suburbs, I believe it was an attempt to make one's house special because all the houses looked the same. Dun Roaming was a popular choice, and one neighbor of the Walkers called their house after their children, beginning with Valerie, then Valavril, and finally Valavlynn. What a chore for the postman to have to learn all these names.

One other happening of note was when I was bought the most beautiful white lace dress and given a poem to learn for a celebration organized by the British Legion to honor those who died in the First World War. I stood on stage and recited John McCrae's famous poem, *In Flanders Fields* while holding a tray of red poppies representing the flowers that grew in abundance in the fields of Flanders and covered the graves of fallen soldiers. Poppies are still worn today throughout the Commonwealth on November 11, known as Remembrance Day. As I recited the last line, "We shall not sleep, though poppies grow in Flanders Fields", I scattered the poppies and added, "We will remember them". I loved the dress and wore it until I could no longer squeeze intuit.

Life at my school began to change as I heard more and more about something called the Eleven Plus. This was a public exam all eleven-year-olds would sit and had enormous consequences for the futures of the children. Those who passed would go on to grammar schools, where the emphasis was on academics, and would lead to careers or further education. Those who failed would attend so-called secondary moderns where the emphasis would be more on practical skills, and would leave at fifteen to enter the work force. Except for severe illness or other extenuating circumstances, retaking the exam was not allowed. Parents understood well the importance of this exam and children were bribed with promises of new bikes if they passed.

Cross Gates Primary had a brilliant teacher who was famous for the high percentage of her pupils passing the exam and she began to drill us daily in the skills and knowledge we needed to be successful. She had a nice sense of humor and once teased us with a trick question: Which is heavier a pound of lead or a pound of feathers? Of course, we all said lead and she laughed at us.

As far as I remember, the exam consisted of arithmetic, English, and an intelligence test, and the emphasis was on completing many, many, questions within the allotted time. English currency in those days was very difficult. The metric system was adopted decades later. We had to learn there were twelve pennies in a shilling and twenty shillings in a pound.

The coins consisted of a farthing (quarter of a penny) a halfpenny, a penny, a three-penny bit, a sixpence, a shilling, a half crown (two shillings and sixpence) and pound notes. Guineas (twenty-one shillings) which no longer existed as an actual coin, were often used to price clothes in expensive stores and so we had to learn those absurd calculations too.

For spelling and grammar we studied homonyms and synonyms and learned all the collective nouns of which there were scores, for example, a gaggle of geese, a pride of lions. We also had to explain the meaning of common proverbs, many of which I now realize came from Benjamin Franklin. I liked the intelligence test best because it involved solving puzzles such as working out the answer through a matrix, e.g., placing people correctly around a table if you were given a minimum of information.

The exam took place on one day in the month of

January and I remember how bitterly cold it was waiting for the local bus to take us to the regional testing site. Some of the children were white with fear and one child threw up. They all knew how much was riding on this test. I looked forward with eagerness to the challenge of the exams as I was always top of the class, but I felt terribly sorry for the worried children, knowing instinctively how unfair this process was. Perhaps this was the first sign of empathy in me.

My amazing teacher decided that she wanted me and another bright girl to sit for the exam for a scholarship to the prestigious private school, Leeds Girls' High School. Six scholarships were offered that year, with one of those places going to a fee-paying child and the rest to the schools in the Greater Leeds area. As I recall, the exam consisted of arithmetic and reading comprehension. We both made the short list and had to submit ourselves to a personal interview.

It was an extremely intimidating experience to enter the headmistress's study where she was seated with a panel of strangers who seemed so erudite and did not speak with a Yorkshire accent. When I could not explain the word "sundry" in a piece of Dickens I was reading out aloud to them and wouldn't even guess, I thought I had ruined my chances as too late I remembered my teacher's advice to always try to answer a question. However, sometime later my foster mother received a letter telling me that I had been awarded a scholarship and her only comment was "How are we going to afford the uniform?" At school I learned that the other girl from my school had also been given a scholarship and, in contrast to the reaction of my foster mother, much ado was made out of this extraordinary accomplishment by our primary school, including the immediate granting of a half day holiday in our honor. Later, when I was informed that I had also passed the eleven plus, my foster mother remarked that they had expected that.

Looking back, I realize that although I received attention and even affection from my teachers and was popular with my friends, it was painful and bewildering for me never to receive any praise from my foster parents for anything I achieved. Aunty was dutiful and conscientious and not often unkind. She bought me my first doll and once threw a birthday party for me. But she never joked lightheartedly with me, hugged or kissed me, reserving her affection for her grandchildren. So, when out of the blue my teacher petitioned to adopt me, I was astonished to learn that my foster mother refused to let me go. In my mind, she didn't care for me very much or why would she threaten to send me back to the Home whenever I broke her rules. I seemed to be a nuisance to her, and was constantly being reminded of how much money I cost her. My relationship with my foster parents was a constant puzzle as I struggled to understand why they had chosen to offer me a home in the first place.

The teacher's offer (interestingly enough, I don't even recall her name or much about her) bewildered me too. We were close in the way that a child would be if singled out for special attention by an adult, but she was still a teacher and in my unformed mind, teachers belonged in school and it was impossible for me to imagine her as having any kind of reality outside the classroom. This is a common perception of young children (I remember my son Richard at three years old being amazed to run across his nursery school teacher in the grocery store), and it indicates to me how very immature I was at the age of eleven, and how circumscribed my interaction with the larger world had been. But that was soon to change dramatically as I headed out to join the Upper Third at Leeds Girls' HighSchool.

Leeds Girls' High School

Leaving my small, single story primary school, with its concrete playground and planted firmly in the middle of a public housing estate, to attend my new high school located in Headingly, a well-to-do section in northwest Leeds, brought enormous changes to my life. For one thing, I no longer played with my local friends as we all scattered to different schools and spent most of our evenings doing homework. Secondly, Leeds Girl's High School seemed enormous to me, with its three elegant buildings housing pupils from kindergarten to sixth form and surrounded by beautiful grounds that included tennis courts, a swimming pool and sports fields. Most special of all was an exquisite library with handcrafted English oak furniture on which the artist Robert Thompson had carved his signature mice.

And of course, there was the green and white uniform. This consisted of a tunic, white blouse, green tie, green cardigan or pullover, green knickers, brown "sensible" shoes and white socks and the universally hated green hat. In the summer, we wore sandals,floral short sleeved dresses, a blazer and of course the dreaded hat. For gym and other sports, we wore a white shirt and the knickers, or grey shorts if we preferred which usually happened when a girl started her period.

The uniform (except for the hat) was a source of pride for me as it identified me as belonging to a particular tribe, enabling me to fit in and giving me a sense of belonging. It also had its downside since the public could easily recognize our school affiliation and any slight breaking of the rules once off school property could be reported. Offences that were frowned upon were not wearing the hat, eating on the bus, hanging about in the city center instead of going straight home, and being rowdy, pushy, noisy, or rude.

Once we reached the fifth form, we could exchange the tunic for a skirt and even though technically we all looked the same, it was amazing how certain girls managed to look so much better in uniform than others. Cosmetics were forbidden, of course, but with a slight wisp of eye shadow and the tiniest hint of lipstick, together with a flounced petticoat, they transformed themselves into a much more attractive version of the rest of us while technically following the rules!

Another great change was no longer being able to walk to school. To get to LGHS I had to get up early to take a tram into central Leeds, and then change to another that would take me northwest to Headingly. I loved double-decker trams and since my stop was one away from the terminus, I could go to the front of the top deck to get the best view and be reasonably assured of finding an empty seat. The only disadvantage was that smoking was allowed on the top deck and sometimes the air would become unbearable as more people came upstairs. When London got rid of its trams, bright red with picture windows upstairs, Leeds bought many of them and my pleasure was doubly increased. If the next tram sitting at the terminus was the old kind, I would ignore it as it clanged by my stop and wait for the red one.

Although most of the girls attending the school spoke with a Yorkshire accent and so in that sense I blended in immediately, they all came from middle class homes and had experiences that I could barely comprehend. When our form mistress asked each of us in turn where we had spent our summer holidays, I was nervous about mentioning staying in a caravan in Bridlington after hearing others talking about the likes of the beautiful resort of Torquay in Devon, the Lake District, and even France.

Because the pupils were drawn from all over the greater Leeds area and evenings were always spent with family and homework, there was at least among the younger girls very little socializing with school friends. So the fact that we all wore the same uniforms and did not visit each other after school made it easier for me to be accepted as an equal. Certainly, there was no prejudice against scholarship girls since we had earned our place based on our brains not because of some special outreach to the poor.

The other scholarship girl lived only a street away from me but we were never close friends, I suspect because she always saw me as a rival. Instead I formed two friendships that have lasted me a lifetime: Margaret Watson, the daughter of a Leeds chemist, and Rosalind Niblett, the daughter of a professor at Leeds University. Neither Rosalind nor I can pinpoint the time when we became fast friends but our closeness was based on mutual attraction whereas my friendship with Maggie, a dainty girl barely five feet tall, (and my partner in crime) like many friendships formed in school was due to purely random circumstance. According to a bizarre long-standing custom, each class lined up by height, the tallest girl leading off, as we all marched every day into morning assembly. Maggie was the shortest girl and I was next. Sometime during the first year I had a big growth spurt and my form mistress finally took note.

"My goodness," she said, "What are you doing at the end of the line?" and moved me to the middle. But by then our friendship had been cemented and neither separation for morning assembly, nor later being placed in different classes did anything to affect our bond.

Our forced separation to different forms in the Lower Fourth was due to our propensity to get into many scrapes. I'd grown up eagerly reading countless adventure stories in which high spirited girls became admired for pulling off daring acts and so on a much more trivial level I tried to emulate my heroines. I was the ring leader and Maggie was my willing partner.

Escaping from school during the lunch hour which was strictly forbidden was our main daring challenge. On one such escapade, we headed down the main road to a baker's shop where we intended to use our lunch money for cream buns. While we were in the shop, we noticed a prefect lurking outside. It was a Wednesday, half day closing, and we begged the shopkeeper to let us stay inside until the prefect gave up on us and went off back to school. Little did we know that the science teacher, stern Miss Lefevre, was also in the shop and she promptly marched us back to school in disgrace. There were many such occasions when my giggling friends observed me sitting on a bench outside the headmistress's office, waiting to be summoned. Amazingly, fifty years later, that bench was still there.

One time I was wrongly accused of bullying a younger girl. Apparently the girl named a person called Spam as the chief perpetrator of the nasty teasing and it had taken the teachers a while to track me down as the owner of that nickname. I was indignant and told the headmistress that while I was aware of some of the teasing of this girl, mostly because she had a posh London accent, I had played no part in it. On a previous occasion, I had refused to name a third party who had been involved with one of my pranks and had escaped detection. This act of not ratting on my co-conspirator probably led the headmistress to consider me an ethical person in spite of my naughtiness and so thank goodness my truthful denial of the bullying was accepted. In fact, it was not a question of ethics. I was simply copying the behavior of my fictional heroines who I felt sure would have never divulged the names of their co-conspirators.

Finally, my form mistress, a quiet but firm lady and one of the few teachers who was married, sat me down to talk about my naughtiness. She told me that she saw I was popular and a natural leader and that I could use these strengths to set a fine example to my fellow pupils or waste my gifts on these silly escapades. I was astonished that someone took the trouble to address my faults in any other way but with sternness and punishment and resolved to live up to her high expectations of me. That is not to say I became a perfectly behaved child. Taking a short cut across the exquisite parquet floor of the assembly hall for example, which was strictly forbidden, instead of going the longer way around to class, was too tempting to resist, especially when late for class!

Leeds Girls' High School was patterned in part on the boys' public schools.[1] It was the first girls' day school in England to adopt the house system for the purpose of fostering competition in sports and other areas. The houses were named after the four patron saints: St. George of England, St. Andrew of Scotland, Saint David of Wales, and St. Patrick of Ireland. On our Saint's day, we wore a colored sash (mine was purple as I was in St. Andrew's) and sang an appropriate hymn. Emphasis was made on preparing the girls for whatever life they eventually adopted. It was an all-round education and so in addition to the standard

[1]

---

[1] So called public schools in Britain are in fact private. Those who could read and write were usually monks, and members of the nobility and the wealthy, who had private tutors. Public schools were originally boarding schools established to educate poor scholars.

academic subjects, we were also introduced in the Upper Third (the first class of high school) to French, art, music appreciation, domestic science which included cooking and sewing, dancing (ballroom, and Scottish and English country dancing) and an abundance of sports. There was gymnastics year-round, field hockey and netball in the winter, tennis, rounders (similar to softball and probably the forerunner of American baseball), swimming and athletics in the summer.

Since England has an established church with the monarch as the secular head, scripture was taught in all schools and hymns and prayers were part of the morning assembly. The Jewish girls in our school were exempt from the part of the assembly devoted to singing and praying, but I am not sure about scripture lessons as that took the form of studying the Bible. We were all very bored by scripture, partly because it was never the subject of tests so we had no need to take notes, and because it was taught by our regular teachers who themselves were clearly bored or at least uninspired by their task.

Since we only had female teachers, we were astonished and very intrigued one day to find a male teacher had been hired to teach scripture. He was a minister and obviously used to teaching boys and our excitement at having a man to teach us soon faded. We were outraged at the way he yelled at us, let alone rapping our knuckles with a ruler if we slacked off. Our female teachers were strict but never unkind so we decided to teach him a lesson. At a given signal, each girl one after the other pushed her heavy bible off the desk on to the floor. It made an enormous racket and when he angrily bellowed at us to stop, the poor girl whose turn it was next had to decide whether she dare defy him. In the end we lost our nerve, but we did report him to our teachers and he thankfully disappeared.

The teachers were a mixed bunch of women almost all unmarried and destined to stay that way, but all in all I think they were kind hearted, although we assigned unflattering nicknames to them: Loopy Lawson, the musical appreciation teacher, the Bug (Miss Ellington whose initials were FLE), the rather fierce gym teacher, and Kipper Feet, the flat-footed art teacher. Miss Sykes, the Headmistress, was a rather remote figure who brought her West Highland terrier to school every day and always assigned the Bug to deal with anything unpleasant in assembly, such as the deplorable state of the toilets. The most interesting teacher was a Miss Noakes, who taught Latin. She taught her subject well, was a firm but fair disciplinarian and I grew to admire her.

It did not occur to me to confide in her, or any teacher at school for that matter, when later my life at home began to deteriorate. Teachers, like all adults in authority, seemed unapproachable to me but had I done so, I believe she would have been a sturdy rock in my life. She was built like a man with strong square shoulders and very short hair, and always wore gray suits. She was obviously a lesbian although I doubt if many of us knew that word or concept. We would have called her mannish.

Every Christmas, we had a school dance which gave us a chance to dress up. Since we were an all girls' school, we danced with each other and with our teachers and it was always a matter of curiosity as to what our teachers would wear, especially Miss Noakes. To our astonishment and much amusement, she appeared in a man's dinner jacket and black skirt. The two young teachers, Miss Walker, the art teacher who daringly wore colorful tights, and Miss Boys, the other gym teacher on whom for a while I had a severe crush, were our favorites but alas they soon married and disappeared out of our lives.

During the first year, we were introduced in our biology class to human reproduction. The teacher framed her program around the concept of parental involvement, beginning with amoebas and lowly earthworms where obviously there was none, progressing through birds with enchanting stories of the depths to which both male and female birds worked together to build nests and protect their young from predators, and finally, to the accomplishment of much sniggering, she came to humans. We giggled at the diagrams of male genitalia and were embarrassed at depictions of our own female bodies. At the same time, I think some of us were relieved to learn that the changes we were going through in puberty were normal. Boys had no trouble exposing themselves to each other as they engaged in contests to see who could urinate the highest against a wall for example, but girls in those days kept their bodies well hidden, no breasts falling out of crop tops or pierced navels exposed, and mothers were not always forthcoming about what their daughters should expect as they developed. Parental involvement in the nurturing of their offspring, our teacher intoned, was at the highest level in the animal kingdom, but my thoughts turned sadly to my own parents who had failed spectacularly in that regard.

We realized that we were learning biology but we were not learning about sex, and sex had lurked as a mystery throughout our lives, always present but unexplained. However, when cheeky boys yelled at us across the street that they would put their chips in our fish cakes, we were shocked, and annoyed that we could find no equivalent threat to hurl back at them, but we were also titillated. We occasionally encountered men who exposed themselves to us in parks and we knew that teenagers preferred to sit up in the balcony of the cinema so they could neck.

One of my friends in the neighborhood smuggled one of her parents' books out of the house and we were astonished at the drawings in it of men and women performing sex in a variety of impossible positions. One particular picture showed a male performing a sex act with five females at the same time and we giggled in disbelief and groaned with disgust. I suspect the book was a version of the *Kama Sutra*. In any case, we called it a mucky book since we could not connect that to our belief that sex was something that parents did only in order to have a child.

Curiously enough, I don't remember being much aware of pregnant women, although there were always lots of prams parked outside local shops. Perhaps it was because the women in those days took care to wear baggy clothes that did not reveal their condition until late in pregnancy. Certainly, while pregnancy was an occasion for joy in the family, it was not for public display. My sister told me that when she was expecting her first child, she went with her mother-in-law to a bingo game and offered to go to the bar to pay for a round of drinks for the group. Her mother-in-law grabbed her furiously by the arm and sat her down, saying that she wasn't going to show them up by flaunting her state.

Although I was a reasonably studious child, I also loved physical activity and during recess, when many girls liked to stroll along the terrace and chatter, I usually preferred to be playing some kind of energetic game. My friends and I particularly liked to do handstands and invented different kinds of formations with our legs, Victory V, OXO, Running in Place, and gave each other style points. And of course I adored sports, especially the ones that involved running such as athletics and hockey. When my name was announced at assembly as having scored a goal against another school, my French teacher looked at me in amazement.

"I didn't know you played hockey for the school," she said. "You are so slight; I would think the bigger girls would knock you over."

"Ah, but they have to catch me first," was my uncharacteristically cheeky reply.

On the other hand, swimming was a nightmare for me. I had never had the opportunity to learn to swim and so languished in the shallow end of the pool with Maggie and a few others and envied the girls who swam and dived with abandonment and seemed like sleek otters in the water. A new gym mistress arrived and having set the swimmers to some task, she advanced with a no nonsense look on her face to the shallow end and demanded to know why I couldn't swim.

"I'm afraid I will sink and no one will notice," I confessed.

"Hold your nose and sit on the bottom of the pool," she commanded and not daring to defy her I did just that. To my astonishment, I bobbed right up, unable to stay on the bottom.

"There," she said. "You can't drown so now there is no reason why you can't swim."

After this revelation, it took me very little time to be able to swim a length of the pool. I never became proficient at swimming, although amazingly I actually passed a life-saving test (poor drowning person who had to rely on me!) and eventually was able to swim half a mile. Years later, when I took swimming lessons to keep up with my five-year-olds who were learning the freestyle, my instructor told me she had never met anyone so tense in the water. I gave up and discovered running instead, but that's another story.

My first year ended with a warm sense of having found my place in the new school. I had many friends, I had learned valuable lessons about recognizing and living up to my strengths, my marks in the end of term exams were good (those in French were particularly good which meant I was eligible to study Latin the following year), and I was looking forward to time off from schoolwork and to renewing my friendships with the neighborhood children. A visit from my boarding out officer, Chris Baker, put an abrupt end to my relative contentment.

She came to the house for what I thought was a routine visit. My Aunty, she solemnly informed me, was not well and needed to go away for a holiday to get better. I had not been aware of any illness and I begged to be allowed to go with them. Miss Baker explained that my Aunty needed a complete rest, and so I was to be sent to the Street Lane Home just for a while. The best news, she told me, was that my sister Mary was currently in the Home and so I would have some companionship. And it was only for three weeks.

Something did not ring true and I became even more suspicious when I was told to take all my possessions with me, including my school uniform and text books. I was fearful, remembering what had happened to Mrs. Thomas. Nevertheless, I had learned in my short life to trust and accept blindly all authority figures for who else could I turn to, and there was especially no reason to doubt Miss Baker's word for she had always been kind to me.

There was an air of gloom which I didn't understand as I said a tearful goodbye to my foster parents, who promised to write.

Street Lane Home – 1951

Street Lane Home or Central Home as it was also called, was a large redbrick probationary home and administrative centre erected in 1901 and housed forty children. On arriving at the Home, I surrendered all my possessions including the clothes I was wearing and was given used clothes and shoes to wear. I was then marched off to the recreation room where I was introduced briefly to some of the girls (the boys were away at a holiday camp), and because Mary was away for the day, I was left to fend for myself. I was confused and miserable as the girls ignored me. They were busy making up some kind of dance in preparation for a show they wanted to put on.

After a while, they fell to bickering and turned to me, demanding whether I could dance and to show them what I could do. I froze. I could certainly do the silly steps they were making up but they wanted something original. I could hardly show them the pirouettes and twirls that I had imagined was ballet dancing and in any case I was not even sure they knew what ballet was. There was nothing else I could offer until thank goodness I remembered the handstands. We marched outside and I demonstrated the different types I could do. They became instantly excited by the novelty and under my guidance fell to practicing my inventions. The staff observed us and said we could continue to do the handstands until the boys came back and then it had to stop as they didn't want us showing our knickers!

Later in the day, Mary appeared and I felt a little less lonely and bewildered.

The days were very boring as I recall, mostly spent in playing and talking, and in the evening, darning black stockings which the girls had to wear. I slept in a bed next to Mary in a dormitory of several girls of different ages. The staff came in during the night to haul the bed wetters off to the toilets. The boys eventually returned but we were separated from them most of the time except at meals, although even then we sat on different sides of the dining room.

One day, a woman who I think was probably the wife of the Superintendent, appeared in the dining room and a hush fell on the children as if they expected something momentous and frightening was about to happen. She dragged a small girl in front of the assembled children and rubbed her face in a urine soaked sheet as a punishment for wetting the bed. I was horrified, and judging by the rumblings of outrage all around me, so were the children.

"She can't help it." they muttered, understanding as I did that no child would deliberately wet her bed and face certain punishment. The children instinctively knew, though they may not have known how to put in so many words, that those in the home were already deeply traumatized by their personal stories and this public punishment served no purpose but to humiliate and destabilize the child further. They also knew full well that the punishment would not produce the desired effect of a dry night and that the child was in for more harsh treatment.

Years later, Mary gave me an example of a punishment she endured. The local people had a habit of taking some of the children out for a treat – a trip to the theater, a picnic, or to their home. Sometimes the staff chose the child and sometimes the neighbors requested a particular child and Mary was on such a visit when I first arrived. She was apparently very popular and was often selected by the locals, which for some reason annoyed the Superintendent's wife. The staff kept special clothes and shoes for the children to wear for these outside visits but Mary recalls that she was deliberately given some old shoes with holes in them. When she returned to the Home, the Superintendent's wife pointed to the holes and blamed Mary. In a fit of rage, she chased her around the room, slapping at her with the offending shoes. Rumor had it that the Superintendent and his wife were eventually sacked and sent to prison for their sadistic behavior, but I have not been able to confirm that.

Not all the staff was unkind. Sometimes they took the children to a nearby wood where we had a picnic. The place was within walking distance so I think it might have been Roundhay Park, a beautiful recreational area for the people of Leeds. We were compelled to walk in single file (we called it a crocodile), stared at by the local people we passed, until we reached the area where we were allowed to let loose, climbing the big boulders of millstone grit, dabbling in the stream, or just running free. The food was bread and dripping and stale cake.

Two weeks had passed and I had heard nothing from my foster parents and so wrote to them asking when I was coming home but got no reply. I wonder now if the staff ever sent the letter, knowing something I didn't. A few days later, the staff planned another picnic. I absolutely loathed the whole ritual of marching in formation in our black stockings through the neighborhood so when a request was made for a volunteer to stay behind and scrub the huge kitchen floor, I eagerly offered to do the job.

On that day, a Mrs. Whitaker and her daughter Susan appeared at the Home requesting to interview Mary. She and her husband were potential foster parents and were looking for a girl one year older than their daughter who was ten years old at the time. The staff explained that Mary was away on a picnic but her older sister was available. Mrs. Whitaker made it clear that she had no interest in a twelve-year-old until the staff member, looking at Susan's blazer, mentioned that I too attended Leeds Girls' High School. Understandably, Mrs. Whitaker was quite astonished and asked for me to be brought to her. Later, I was told I was to spend the day with this family, but suspecting nothing I readily agreed. I thought it was just another example of a family wanting to give a child a treat, a chance to get out of the Home and into a regular family for the day.

Whether it was the next day, or if not certainly soon thereafter, I was summoned to the office and there was my boarding out officer, Miss Baker. She took me aside and explained that I was never going back to the Walkers. Mrs. Walker was too ill, but never mind, here was a nice family willing to take me and even better, the daughter went to the same school. And it would all be settled before school started in the autumn. I was absolutely devastated. Not only had the Walkers and I believe the staff at the Home deceived me, but my one true rock, Miss Baker, had colluded with them and blatantly lied to me. And by presenting me with the awful truth on the one hand and offering me this escape from the Home on the other, all wrapped up so to speak in a neat package, they really gave me no choice. Miss Baker, with whom I became great friends later in life, told me that it was the worst moment of her career and she always bitterly regretted her deception. The Walkers had begged and pleaded with her not to tell me the truth as I headed for the Home, and she had finally broken down and agreed to be a party to their lie.

Leeds Girls High School, 1951, left to right, Rosalind Niblett, friend, Margaret Watson, me, friend

At a birthday party, me in the front with Maggie to my right.

At school, showing off my handstand

Chapter 4: 14, Moorland Rise, Leeds
1951-1954
12-15 years old

Phillip and Beatrice Whitaker had grown up in the rough and tumble of working class neighborhoods but when Mr. Whitaker became a clerk at the central branch of the Midland Bank in City Square, they moved to the Moortown area of Leeds and entered the middle class. A bank clerk in those days was a respected and fairly prestigious job and I believe he had a rather senior position. He was so conscientious, that even though he was diabetic, he insisted on staying late to go over the accounts if there were some discrepancies in the balances and occasionally, forgetting to eat, he would go into a diabetic coma. He was a chronic smoker with a dreadful cough, but he was a kind man although again somewhat elusive and certainly no father figure that I could attach to.

 It had taken them eight years to finally have a child and so not surprisingly Susan was spoilt.

 Mrs. Whitaker was an attractive looking woman, strong-minded, controlling and mercurial in temperament and somewhat of a snob. She reveled in her elevation to the middle class, which she demonstrated in many ways, but especially on Election Day when she walked to the polling station with her British bulldog, the very symbol of conservatism in Britain and the well-known nickname for Winston Churchill. Snuffy, decked out in red, white and blue rosettes, signaled to all that she was voting for the Conservatives, not the Labour party of the working class. She sent her daughter to an expensive private school, and bizarrely insisted on the use of certain words she thought genteel such as "saline" instead of salty.

She was a great cook, especially brilliant at bakery items and conscientiously weighed every ingredient so she knew exactly how much sugar her diabetic husband was eating. For the first time in my life I was not hungry and it was, at least in the beginning, very satisfactory for Mrs. Whitaker to cater to such a healthy eater. Susan, on the other hand, was a fussy eater, using food to gain a modicum of control over her strong-willed mother. She was also an introvert and much preferred sedentary occupations such as crayoning or reading than being outside engaged in physical activity.

So, into this household I came, seared by the Walkers' deception and uncertain where my future lay. The Whitakers made it clear from the start that my role was to be a companion to Susan and, in some way, I was grateful for their honesty because it did not raise my expectations by leading me to hope that I might eventually become an equal in the family. Later, I played very different roles, but at least at the start things were tolerable. I liked Susan and was quite prepared to be a friend and mentor. The problem for Mrs. Whitaker was much as she loved her daughter, she was constantly irritated and frustrated by Susan's fussiness. To make matters worse, I was much more like the child she had been growing up - good at sports, able to handle balls and skipping ropes, steeped in the traditional rhyming games, and a sound sleeper with a healthy appetite - none of which applied to Susan. On top of this, I had won a scholarship to Susan's school.

Mrs. Whitaker had a cruel side to her and occasionally she responded to Susan's whining or refusal to eat by unleashing a barrage of abusive words which would last for a long time and sometimes ended in Susan getting a slap. Susan would cry pitifully and then her mother would hug Susan and beg for forgiveness. Another example of Mrs. Whitaker's cruelty was when Susan's canary died. Snuffy the bulldog had started to show aggressive tendencies and had been put to sleep and so in its place Susan was given a canary. It sang beautifully, especially when the kettle was boiling, and we all loved it. Then it died and Susan cried her heart out. Mrs. Whitaker, impatient with her daughter's reaction, grabbed the dead bird and threw it on the fire. It was an insensitive act and I felt immensely sorry for Susan.

In the same vein, she had a great preference for books about Japanese war camps and would read out portions to me with relish about Japanese soldiers engaging in sadistic acts with women and babies. I believe now that Mrs. Whitaker was sexually frustrated. Apart from the nasty books she enjoyed, she also inexplicably decided to take us one afternoon to the Leeds City Varieties, a well-known old fashioned Victorian music hall. In its heyday, it was a very famous theatre featuring such performers as Charlie Chaplin and Houdini, but in the early 50's the whole place seemed seedy, with the only other people in the audience being a few old men in raincoats – the stereotype of dirty old men characters. What on earth were we young girls doing there?

The show was mostly various song and dance acts and really corny comedians with a slightly risqué flavor to their jokes. One such joke told about a woman who went to buy oranges and was told that they were reserved for pregnant women. She replied that she would be back the next day. I understood the point of the joke (I'm sure Susan didn't), but was still puzzled why that was very funny. The show ended with what most people were seemingly waiting for - a woman posing naked. Because of the laws at that time, women could only be shown naked on stage if they didn't move. This woman was shown in various poses that represented the names of newspapers. The only one I can remember was *The Daily Worker* which she depicted by posing naked with a shovel in her hand!

Mrs. Whitaker also directed her anger and frustration at me but I gave her no satisfaction. I would stand there defiantly, tuning her out, and when I got slapped, I refused to cry, at least in her presence.

Around the time when I was between the ages of thirteen and fourteen, Mrs. Whitaker decided she would like to find the place in Leeds where I grew up and see if we could track down any relatives. I have no idea what her motives were but off we went. Wilson Court was exactly as I had remembered except the pig sties were no longer there. We went into the butcher's shop on the corner and the owner confirmed that there had been pigs but some kind of incendiary in the war had destroyed them. We knocked at the door of Number 3 and an unkempt woman with a small girl clinging to her long skirt answered the door. I was riveted by the sight, feeling that I was staring at myself as I must have looked years ago.

We crossed the Wellington Road and climbed the hill towards to Renton Place, where my grandparents lived. As we approached the house, an old man was leaving the outdoor toilet and heading for this house. It was my grandfather. He told us that my grandmother had died of cancer and that my three aunts all lived nearby. After that we left. I asked no questions and I could not feel any remote emotional connection to what I just seen or experienced. It was as though I was looking at someone else's life. And I certainly had no desire to restart any relationship with this family; sorting out my feelings about the people I currently lived with was hard enough. Perhaps I also recognized that the changed circumstances of my life since being torn from Wilson Court had made a huge gulf between me and my birth family.

If my grandmother had been alive, I might have had a different reaction to seeing her again, as I still had warm memories of her attempt to keep the family together, but those memories did not extend to my grandfather or aunts. Perhaps, too, my lack of connection was because the visit had been driven by Mrs. Whitaker's curiosity rather than by any kind of desire by me to find my roots. What did thrill me was the confirmation that all my memories of where I had lived had proved to be accurate. The location of Wilson Court, the pigs, the bombed house, the railway line, the canal, Armley Gaol, and my grandparent's house were exactly as I remembered, and that surely meant that other memories about events and conversations were probably reliable too. Many people claim to remember conversations and events in their lives when in fact they are remembering what other people related to them and through time they embrace them as their own. In my case there was no one to tell me these stories, no continuous thread of family lore, so I believe my memories are real.

Looking at photographs taken during the first year of my life with the Whitakers, one might guess that I had found a stable and happy home. These pictures show me and the Whitaker family engaging in country walks, enjoying the seaside and celebrating Susan's birthday with friends of my own. But it became very clear fairly early on that my role in the Whitaker family was changing rapidly into something I resented and eventually couldn't tolerate.

The hardest thing was that being a companion to Susan meant I was forbidden to have friends of my own so could not accept invitations unless Susan was included. And I had no privacy. I had somehow acquired a diary and felt a strong urge as many teenage girls do to write down my intimate thoughts as I saw my body changing, and experienced the struggle to make great adjustments to yet another family with its different rules and ideas of what it thought important. I did not trust that they would honor my privacy, so I wrote a test paragraph in the diary in code. As I suspected, Mrs. Whitaker tried to decipher it, and when she couldn't solve the code, asked Susan to do it. Although it was a simple substitution code, she was not able to decipher it either and so Mrs. Whitaker blew up at me for what she described as despicable behavior. I told her that a diary was supposed to be private and refused to translate the paragraph. It was a small victory for me but I didn't continue with the diary.

The second change in my role was that I had to do many chores. At the beginning, Susan and I shared these duties. One of the jobs was to "do the dishing", i.e. placing a chamber pot and a glass of water by the side of each bed and emptying them in the morning. Soon that became my job entirely. Another job was to clean all the brass. Mrs. Whitaker was exceptionally fond of brass and had a row of horse brasses across the wall above the mantelpiece. She also had a brass holder for the fire utensils, a large bucket to hold the coal, and a fender, all of which needed to be cleaned every week. It was a tiresome and smelly job and soon Susan refused to do it. I was made to do the job on Saturday mornings and had to have it finished if I wanted to go to the Saturday morning picture show. Eventually, Susan complained of the smell in the house and I was banished to the garage, which was very cold in winter. Having to do chores at the age of twelve is neither terrible nor unusual, but it was the way I was made to do these jobs that caused me to feel such resentment. For one thing, Susan was gradually excluded from all chores, hardly a recipe for forging the strong bonds between us that Mrs. Whitaker initially seemed to want. I also felt that if I as the older girl had to do all the chores, then there should be some privilege or reward attached to that, not only as an incentive for me to do a good job without resentment, but also as a model for Susan. In fact, I was made to feel as an outsider or a maid, and thanks and appreciation were never expressed.

The issue of money and how much I was costing them came up frequently, as it did with Mrs. Walker. I was reminded by a resentful Mrs. Whitaker that Susan's gifts from relatives at Christmas time were not as generous because they had to include me in their spending. I could find no answer to this but the guilt at costing people money remained with me for a very long time. The only Christmas present I can remember receiving was a dressing table set similar to the one Mrs. Walker had, but it had been bought at the Leeds market and was chipped and cracked. A secondhand gift for a secondhand child!

But the real bitter souring of the relationship came when Susan failed to win a scholarship to Leeds Girls' High School and it was decided that she should go to the local grammar school. From that day on, jealousy drove Mrs. Whitaker and she did her best to isolate me further from my friends and school activities, belittling my school, and forcing me to check Susan's homework every night to make sure that she got good marks while my own homework suffered. Susan would be praised for receiving all A's, and I was mocked for only managing B's. If she failed to get an A, I was accused of deliberately sabotaging her.

Susan at eleven had not been told any of the facts of life, so when my first period arrived at the age of thirteen, there was a question of how I would manage this without rousing Susan's curiosity. I knew that my friends, most of whom had already started menstruation, used sanitary pads bought from the local chemist. To my horror, Mrs. Whittaker presented me with squares of old toweling which I was to use as napkins. I was consumed with agony that everyone at school would detect the bulkiness under my tunic and I was also worried that wearing one napkin all day would be smelly and people would be aware of this. Because Susan would ask what these squares of cloth were for, I was once again sent off to the garage to wash them out and hang them up. And later, when all my friends were wearing bras, Mrs. Whitaker refused to buy me one. Admittedly, I was a slender girl and probably didn't yet need one, but wearing a bra was a rite of passage. It made one feel grown up.

When you wore your white blouse without a cardigan, the bra straps were visible through the material and I didn't want girls to notice that yet again I was the only girl who was different. A friend gave me one of her bras, but Mrs. Whitaker found it in the bottom drawer of my dresser and made me give it back.

More humiliations were to follow. As I grew, I needed new uniform. Although the Whitakers had been given a uniform allowance for me, they evidently decided to make some money on the side. My raincoat came not from the official school outfitters, but from the clothing stall in the Leeds market and then was dyed dark green as a poor approximation of the uniform. When I was old enough to wear a skirt instead of a tunic, Mrs. Whitaker converted my old tunic into a skirt which looked nothing like the real uniform and I was excruciatingly embarrassed. We started tennis and I was the only one without a racquet. The gym mistress found one for me in a box of old equipment. The frame of the one she dug out was completely bent but I had no choice but to learn with that. I have friends who love to stand out from the crowd in the way they dress or style their hair. I yearned to fit in with the crowd, never to be noticed or pitied for the things I didn't have; only wanting to stand out in academics and sports. I was lucky that I was popular, because my strange life circumstances might well have made me a victim of bullying.

During the disintegration of my relationship with the Whitakers, Rosalind became my close friend and comforter. She and I walked the half mile or so to my bus stop every day and she listened to my woes with a sympathetic ear. I told her that I was not allowed to attend any school activities beyond normal school hours if Susan could not be involved, so when my school competed in a radio academic quiz show, I was not there to join in the excitement. Later, when it was discovered I had some talent for acting and my English teacher wanted to cast me as Miranda in Shakespeare's *The Tempest* – a tremendous honor since it was usually only the senior girls who were chosen for the main parts - Mrs. Whitaker said no. And when I asked if I could go and watch my school's first eleven hockey team play Susan's school, she not only said no, but let forth one of her hysterical rants. When she had finished, I calmly told her that Rosalind was waiting outside the door and I would let her know the answer. Mrs. Whitaker was chagrined because she realized that my friend had heard the whole tirade, but the damage had been done and she could not extricate herself from the situation. It was relief to me that Rosalind heard the abuse and could understand more clearly the strain I was under.

There was a further incident which was yet another turning point in the already poisonous family dynamics. Susan's school did not have its own swimming pool so Mrs. Whitaker was very jealous that during the summer term I took swimming lessons and had great fun in the pool. She tried her best to come up with reasons why I should not swim and one day the excuse was that I had a cold. This was admittedly a legitimate reason but I was furious at not being able to participate yet again in something I loved, so when Rosalind offered to lend me her swimming costume, I took up her offer and went swimming. I had very thick hair in two plaits and the swimming cap always leaked so at the end of the lesson, the last one before going home, my hair was very wet. Rosalind and I dried it off as best we could, putting my plaits through the wringer to squeeze out the water.

Needless to say, Mrs. Whitaker's eagle eye spotted the damp hair and asked if I had been swimming. I do not know why I chose to lie by telling her my hair was wet because I had been fooling with my friends around the water fountain. She did not believe me and launched one of her rants. Once committed to the lie, I couldn't change my story. The verbal attack went on for hours with threats by Mrs. Whitaker to call my gym teacher to find out the truth. Finally, Mr. Whitaker, fed up with the whole thing, remarked in his quiet way that if I said I didn't swim, she should accept it as the truth and let it be. I was flabbergasted and horrified. Here was someone giving me the benefit of the doubt, trusting me when in fact I had lied. I couldn't bear to keep up the deception any longer and immediately confessed and then had to listen to a long lecture about honesty. After that, I became the scapegoat whenever anything went wrong, and when I defended myself, this lie was brought up as proof that I could not be trusted to tell the truth. But when a leather key holder had strangely been found in the toilet and I was blamed for it, I had an answer and it was immensely liberating for me. I told them that I had not done it, had no reason to do it, which could only mean that one of them was lying and therefore they could no longer claim the moral ground of superior honesty.

Now I was beginning to fight back.

By this time, things had become much worse and Mrs. Whitaker took delight in humiliating me. Shoes bought for me from the second hand stall in the market were often too big for me, but I was forced to wear them and it gave Mrs. Whitaker the chance to taunt me about having large feet. While I was doing the chores upstairs, nasty things were said about me which I could hear. And once, when Mrs. Whitaker had to attend to Susan, who had trouble getting to sleep, she looked down at me and let loose a jealous tirade as though the fact that I was asleep was some kind of crime. Of course I was not asleep but I did not want to give her the satisfaction of knowing it. Now my healthy appetite and good sleeping habits were no longer a source of satisfaction to her but something to berate me about.

Things came to a head when Mrs. Whitaker, enraged at something I had done or said, pushed me out of the house, told me not to come back, and locked the door. I was furious and deciding to take her at her word, went into the garage and stayed there all night. It was cold and there was nothing but newspapers to cover myself with but I was determined not to come out of the garage until someone asked me. That someone was a social worker who had been summoned by Mrs. Whitaker, who suddenly all sweetness and light, graciously produced tea and biscuits served in the rarely used lounge. She said it had been foolish of me to stay in the garage because of course she had unlocked the kitchen door before she went to bed, and in any case it was no hardship to sleep in the garage.

I had a strong sense that the social worker (Miss Baker was away) on hearing my side of the story was sympathetic to me and I learned later that she had found Mrs. Whitaker to be neurotic and unstable.

Sometime during my childhood, the authorities in charge of the foster program decided that it would be beneficial for children who had been separated from their siblings to meet with their brothers and sisters from time to time. We gathered in a dreary room in the Children's Office located in a depressing black Victorian building with a clock tower near Woodhouse Moor. I only remember meeting once a year but my siblings knew we met more regularly. My brother John documented thirteen such meetings.

Well-meaning as this was, I questioned the usefulness of seeing John and Mary in such surroundings as a way of bonding with them. Although I had been with Mary in the Home for a few weeks, she was a lot closer to John with whom she had shared foster homes in the past. Mary remembers these meetings and said she and John felt they had nothing in common with me. It was very boring for us because there was nothing to do, but the foster mothers enjoyed it because they exchanged war stories. It must have been helpful for them to learn what each other had experienced.

It was to this same building that Mary, John and I were summoned out of the blue to meet our father who, nine years after the disintegration of the family, petitioned to meet with us. I was deeply suspicious of this meeting because our father had never once attempted to communicate with us in the intervening years. Pondering why he had suddenly developed an interest in us, I came to the conclusion that he must have known that I was fourteen and assumed that when I reached fifteen, I would leave school and earn my living. I doubt he had any idea that I was a scholarship girl attending Leeds Girls' High School. Nevertheless, I reluctantly agreed to give my father the benefit of the doubt, although to be honest I don't think I had a choice. Mrs. Whitaker taunted me that I might want to go back to him.

The meeting with my father was disastrous. He was a tall, thin blonde man with high cheek bones and I could see at once that Mary and I had inherited some of his genes, not a comforting thought as there was nothing to like about the man. He had no warmth. He didn't seem like a father, or how I imagined a father would be. He asked no questions about our welfare or even how we had survived the intervening years. I don't remember that he even hugged us or explained the long silence on his part. He did not talk about our brother Barry. Instead he boasted about his exploits in the war and then launched into a long criticism of our mother, blaming her for everything. I was enraged and disgusted. I had never given much thought as to who should be blamed for my family's disintegration, but my father's diatribe about my mother switched my allegiance totally to her side and I began to make excuses in my mind for her behavior.

The purpose of the meeting was indeed to claim us back and I immediately said no. Bad as things were with the Whitakers, I could not see myself living with this man whose claim to the rights of fatherhood I rejected. I had lived a long time without a father and I knew instinctively that living with this man would damage even further my hopes of relating to a father figure.

Poor Mary responded differently. The only foster family that she had really bonded with had emigrated to Canada and the authorities had refused to let her go with them, apparently because there were some issues of violent behavior connected with the father. Mary was shattered by this loss, and after that was never able to settle down with any family for long. We once counted up that she had lived in thirteen different foster homes including the Home. When she reached eighteen years old, she no longer qualified for foster homes or orphanages so she lived at the YWCA and worked at the Leeds central post office.

So, at thirteen and in yet another unsatisfactory home, she jumped at the chance to live with her real father. I warned her about his motives but her fantasy of returning to her birth family was about to be realized and she would not listen. She moved in with him and his second wife on a six-month trial basis and within few days knew she had made a disastrous choice. She pleaded with the authorities to take her back to the Home, but they were adamant she had to complete the six months. It was a period in Mary's life that she looks back on with horror as she recounts many stories of his abusive and cruel behavior.

She remembers for example how she had been sitting on a tram with her father when he taunted her with the fact that only a few minutes ago her mother had been on the same tram and had just got off at the last stop. He also got angry with her when she asked what had happened to Norma, the baby of the family. Although she didn't remember Norma herself, I had told her about this baby and she was confused when he told her no such child existed. There were many other painful stories but Mary prefers to share them only with me. Needless to say, I took no pleasure in being right about his character, and her stories only served to increase my loathing of him.

John had a similar experience while Mary was living with her real father. John went to visit her and asked our father if he had any photographs of our mother he could spare. This request was greeted with such anger that John fled and did not contact him again.

All three of us had yearned for childhood pictures. Without them, we felt unconnected. If we were to have children of our own someday, we wanted to be able to delight in the genetic links of appearance and mannerisms these pictures would reveal.

In the summer term, after I had turned fifteen, there was much talk about the O (ordinary) Levels - standard examinations prepared and graded by a group of universities. These would take place the following year and those who did well would most likely go on to study for the advanced level exams and then on to university. I barely knew what a university was but the teachers talked to me as though it was a foregone conclusion that I would go and I knew instinctively that it was something that should be part of my future. When I casually mentioned it to Mrs. Whitaker there was outrage. Not only was I not going to university, she shrieked, but I was to leave school at sixteen, after O levels, and work for a living so I could repay them for all the money they had spent on me. Something finally snapped in me. A stream of past ugly scenes with this malicious woman swept through my mind and the fear of being limited all my life by this family struck me so forcibly that I was compelled to action. I made up my mind immediately that I had to get out of this dreadful situation even if the only possibility for me was to return to the awful Home. Anything would be better than suffering the constant emotional abuse. I told her I would be late coming home from school the next day as I was going to see Miss Baker.

My boarding out officer was not surprised by my stories but begged me to hold on until they could find another home for me. I tried my best to get through the next few days with the Whitakers but the fact that I had seen Miss Baker only made them angrier at me. Finally, I had had enough and called Miss Baker again, asking her to take me away. She was in a panic because the three-day Whitsuntide weekend was coming up and she was going on holiday. She called her neighbors, the Christophersons, to see if they would be willing to take me for three days until she got back. They had two boys ages seven and eleven and had been consulting Miss Baker about the possibility of adopting a girl who would bridge the age gap between the two, so I believe she was confident they would help out. They agreed to my temporary stay with them and Miss Baker arrived at the Whitaker's to take me away. My pitiful few possessions were put into a very small suitcase and at the last moment Mrs. Whitaker handed me some of her family photographs. I departed with my head held high and my heart beating painfully while Mrs. Whitaker and Susan sobbed.

In Bridlington, on holiday with
Susan and Mrs. Whitaker, 1952

Feeding the pigeons at Sewerby
Park, Bridlingotn

More in Sewerby Park

In the garden at Moorland Rise

Chapter 5: 6, Oakfield Terrace, Headingly
1954
Age 15

It was a very hot day when I arrived at this Victorian terrace house in Headingley, situated about halfway between my school and Rosalind's home. Mrs. Christopherson, along with her young son James, Betty the au pair girl from France, and Nikki, the charming cat, greeted me with kindness and concern. The older boy, Oliver, was away at Worcester College for the Blind and Professor Christopherson had gone up to London for a meeting and would be back later in the day. Noting my tense, tired face, she suggested I unpack my few things and take a relaxing bath and after that we would have tea on the lawn.

During the tea, Professor Christopherson arrived. I had never met a professor so in my ignorance, (and probably thanks to the sort of books I had read), I imagined him to be a stern, elderly man with a beard, apt to pontificate when he emerged from time to time from his deep philosophical thoughts, so I was unprepared for this young, slim man with a kind demeanor and a twinkle in his eye. He obviously noticed my stress and decided to make me laugh by reciting a funny poem. What followed was a scene I'll never forget. Of all things, he chose to recite *Albert and the Lion,* a well-known poem and favorite party piece about a lad who gets eaten by a lion, occasionally forgetting the words which I then had to supply, and all in an excruciatingly false Northern accent. As I ate my tea and observed this family, I felt I had stepped into the bizarre world of *Alice in*

Wonderland. Had he quoted from Shakespeare, it would have fitted nicely into my idea of how posh cultured people behave, so his choice seemed very strange. I wasn't sure at first if he was mocking me by trying, poorly in my view, to imitate my accent, but then I finally understood he was a kind man who was simply trying to put me at ease by reciting what would be familiar to me, and perhaps letting me know at the same time that he had taken the trouble to learn the words to a famous local poem.

There was a nugget of truth in my expectation that a professor would be an older man, because as I learned later the term designated the head of a university department. Derman Christopherson had left the University of Cambridge to become Professor of Mechanical Engineering at Leeds University at the age of thirty-three, the youngest professor in the UK at that time. Frances Christopherson had been a trained Froebel teacher and was now a full-time housewife. James was a solemn little boy of seven who confused me by speaking like a grownup.

This, I observed, was a family unlike any I had met before. They were a relaxed, untidy group with newspapers and books everywhere, so different from Mrs. Whitaker's rigid and spotless domain that it took some time to adjust, but their warmth and kindness eventually won me over and I began to feel a little more comfortable. I enjoyed their attention and their sense of fun and put aside for the time being thoughts about my future. When my three-day stay was up, Mrs. Christopherson told me that they wanted me to stay and be a permanent part of the family.

This was an enormous dilemma for me. I had been treated very badly by the Whitakers after what had seemed a promising start and I worried how I could make a judgment about my future after a mere three days with this family. And why had they been so quick to embrace me? Was I destined to be a second-class citizen again - a babysitter and housemaid? Could I fit in with an academic family with a lifestyle and value system that might be very different from what I experienced before? Of course, I attended a private girls' school that had given me an entrée into a different world - one that the Christophersons would be familiar with - but I had never been allowed to accept invitations to my friends' homes, so my school experiences gave me only an inkling of what their daily lives must be like.

Weighted against my fear of being exploited and seeing a "honeymoon" period gradually wearing off was the warmth of a family so lacking in guile and calculation, the close proximity of Miss Baker and Rosalind, whose father was a professor at Leeds University and knew the Christophersons, the strong possibility of an active father in my life, and the dread of coping with a return to the Home. I agreed to stay. I learned two things in the next few days: apparently the Christophersons had been enchanted with my exquisite manners (thanks to Mrs. Whitaker), particularly at mealtimes when I always asked permission to leave the table, and Rosalind, in the meantime, had been urging her parents to take me in.

It was a new feeling to be wanted, loved and appreciated and I was giddy.

After another visit to the Children's Welfare Office in that dreary Woodhouse Moor building, my new foster mother thought it would be much nicer to have the get-together in our house. While the foster mothers appreciated her invitation, John and Mary found it a little overwhelming. They were used to having their food served directly for them on their plates (there is even a word for it: "plating.") so when my mother kindly invited them to help themselves to the vegetables in the tureens, they did not know what to do. They did not know what a tureen was or how much to take. In the end, John recalls, I stood up and served him myself to ease his embarrassment.

Once I accustomed myself to James' pedantic way of speaking, I discovered a sweet little boy with a love for dressing up and acting. I did not meet Oliver until he came home from school for the summer holidays but I heard from him. He wrote me a beautiful letter beginning with "Dear Sister." I wish I had kept the letter because it is one of the most precious of my memories. That he could accept a new member of the family without having met her or having been consulted showed a generosity of spirit that I know in similar circumstances I could not have matched.

I learned that Oliver had suffered a detached retina as a child and he and his mother went to Utrecht in the Netherlands for an operation to save the second eye. They lived there for several months, leaving his father to cope with little Jamie. Oliver's eye was saved, although he was still technically blind since, for example, he could only read if he held the book close to his good eye, and so he was enrolled in Worcester

College for the Blind, which I think he enjoyed. His surgeon predicted that his eyesight would last for twenty years but at age seventy he could still see. Much later when I gave it thought, I realized that Jamie in many ways had a tough childhood. First his mother disappeared at a critical age in a toddler's development, then Oliver, whom Jamie adored and tried to keep up with, went off to boarding school, then after a few years of his mother's attention I turned up to soak up a lot of the limelight. In spite of all this, Jamie turned out to be a loving, caring individual.

So began an amazing first year in which the family tried to make up for so many of the normal experiences I had missed throughout my life. They asked me my opinion before they bought me anything. My plaits were cut off and replaced with a stylish hairdo and my hated cheap uniform was tossed in the rubbish bin. I acquired a decent tennis racquet and a new swimsuit. For some reason I yearned for a red shoulder bag and, although it didn't go with any of the few clothes I had, one was bought for me. When a severe streptococci infection caused me to miss the first week of the autumn term, my foster father came back from a trip to London with a gift for me. I was confused because it was not my birthday and I couldn't think of any other reason to receive a present. It was an adorable pale yellow angora beret – all the fashion at the time – and I cherished it not just because it was so pretty and feminine and suited me but what it said about the family.

But it wasn't just about material things. They took turns reading to me at night. They told me jokes and laughed at mine. They celebrated the one year anniversary of my arrival with a special cake, but then sensibly told me they wouldn't continue this in the future because it would not be fair to the other children. They enfolded me in a lighthearted loving embrace and I couldn't get enough.

My eyes were opened by travel. For someone who had never ventured anywhere except to the Yorkshire coast, the day trip to the Yorkshire Dales, the summer holiday in Grasmere in the Lake District, and most eye opening, the half-term trip to London, were events that simply thrilled me and launched me into a lifelong curiosity about other countries andcultures.

We stayed in Raines Park, a rather dreary suburb in South London, with Aunt Mary, my foster father's sister. She was divorced and had one son, John, the same age as I. She taught at the Study, a private school for girls, and took care of her mother, who was becoming increasingly senile. After we did the usual sightseeing – feeding the pigeons in Trafalgar Square, watching the Changing of the Guards at Buckingham Palace - the family returned to Leeds, leaving me to stay two extra days with Aunt Mary. I spent those days, guide book in hand walking around London, breathing in the ancient historical sites. After a while, I noticed a young man following me. Soon he started chatting with me and then invited me to lunch, suggesting we take a taxi. I had no idea how to deal with this. I had been deliberately kept back socially by the Whitakers and attending an all girls' school gave me no experience of dealing with the opposite sex. I wondered if it would be safe but then decided nothing could happen to me in a London taxi and so accepted his invitation. We were dropped off at an Italian restaurant in Knightsbridge, a very elegant part of London. He was a handsome young man from the Middle East and a student at Trinity College in Dublin and obviously very lonely. It was a delightful occasion and we parted with promises to write to each other although I am not sure we ever did.

Aunt Mary gave me my first experience of the London theater. We saw a play called *The Duenna*. She regretted later that she had not made a better choice of play but I was enchanted by the whole evening: the elegant theater resplendent in gold and red velvet in Drury Lane, the ritual of sharing a box of chocolates, and the tea and biscuits that were delivered to us in our seats during the intermission. Added to the fascination with theater going was the fact that I was enjoying for the first time an extended family experience. I now not only had parents, but an aunt who treated me as though I had always been her niece. The trip to London was both the start of my love of travel, and a warm, close relationship with Aunt Mary.

Later, when I traveled to Bremen in Germany as part of a pen pal exchange, I wrote a long rapturous letter home about the trip, describing the crossing on the ferry from the Harwich to the Hook of Holland, the flat landscape that I viewed during the long train ride to Bremen, reminding me of the paintings of Hobbema, stopping at the borders where customs officers came on board looking for smuggled goods, especially coffee which was very expensive in Germany. I wrote about the exotic smells of garlic, salami, and strong coffee, and the chatter in foreign languages, some of which I was beginning to understand.

During my first happy year with the Christophersons (whom I had started calling Mummy and Daddy and referring to them as my parents), I received two surprises that caused me trepidation. First, they announced that they were expecting a baby. They had given up hope of finding a girl to adopt so they decided to try for a third child and had conceived the day before I arrived on their doorstep. Selfishly, I felt a little threatened, worried that a new baby would take away the attention from me, but when Peter Martin was born at the end of February, I adored him from the very first day and became a second mother to him. I had grown to love James and Oliver and to enjoy having brothers, but Peter was very special because, as I told him many times, he and I basically arrived in the family at the same time. I also teased him that had I arrived a day earlier, he might not exist, so he owed me an eternal debt of gratitude!

The second surprise was momentous. Daddy had been offered the job of Professor of Applied Science at Imperial College and we were moving to London. This was a very difficult piece of news for me to absorb. Excited as I had been to visit London, it was Leeds that was the one remaining constant in my life. I loved my city for its many beautiful parks, the shopping arcades and markets (home of the first

Marks & Spencers). Each time I returned from a trip to the exquisite Yorkshire countryside, I was thrilled when we crossed the boundary of Leeds to see the familiar coat of arms depicting a ram, symbol of its famous wool industry. I was proud of the solid black public buildings, churches, and monuments. (It was only later after coal fires had been banned that I discovered that the black color was not the natural stone, but the result of decades of the grime of industrial and domestic pollution. Years later I was astonished to see that after the imposing lions outside City Hall were scrubbed clean, they were a beautiful sandstone color.)

To move at the age of sixteen would be a terrible upheaval, tearing me from my school, my friends, my social worker, and my roots. It also meant that after a little more than a year with this family, I had to decide if I was willing to put my trust in them. The first year with the Whitakers had been pleasant but it had then quickly deteriorated into an antagonistic relationship bordering on abuse. The Christophersons, however, had already anticipated that this huge change would unsettle me. They told me that they knew this would be difficult for me, and had already discussed the situation with the Nibletts, who had offered to let me live with them during the term time and then go home to London for the holidays if I couldn't bear to leave Leeds and my school. The fact that they had thought this through so carefully and considered my needs and feelings made it a little easier to reach the eventual decision to throw my lot in with my new family and move to London.

The summer term was full of stress and excitement. It was stressful because we were sitting for our O levels, those public examinations that would determine to a large extent our futures – good jobs, or continuing with A levels and on to university – and because I was saying goodbye to friends and to my school. But the term also brought the joy of having parents who attended school functions such as Prize Day, and cheered me on Sports Day, watching me win the 100-yard dash, the 220-yard run, anchor my house relay, and win the overall trophy.

During the summer, the Nibletts invited me to join them in Scotland for a family holiday. They met my train in Glasgow and then drove through the hauntingly beautiful valley of Glencoe, the scene of so much slaughter in battles, and on to a rented house in Loch Linnie. The wild beauty of the country, the charm of the Scottish accent, not to mention the sight of a lone piper playing his heart out at the head of one of the passes, thrilled my sentimental soul and I became a lover of all things Scottish.

During our stay, Rosalind and I received the results of our O Level exams. I had done reasonably well and would easily qualify to study French, German and English for A Level at my new school.

Most people left at sixteen after their first exams unless they wanted to study for entry into a university. Classes in the final two years of high school (called the Sixth Form) were therefore quite small and the subjects were taught in depth with lots of individual attention. Rosalind came into her own in the sixth form where a high level of analysis and a more mature understanding of literature rather than rote learning or regurgitating facts were required. In fact, she did brilliantly and won a place at Cambridge University.

Not surprisingly, although I was extremely happy with my new family, not everything had gone smoothly. The Christophersons had no experience with raising a girl, let alone one at the difficult age of fifteen and with a long history of abandonment by the people she trusted. I could be very moody at times and argumentative, particularly about social rules that my new mother tried to enforce. But mostly it was my relationship with my new father that initially caused stress.

I was simply overwhelmed by a man who not only took an active part in my life, but was clearly enchanted by me. He helped me with my math homework, played tennis with me, took me to cricket matches at the famous Yorkshire cricket ground in Headingly and taught me the rules of this complicated game. My love of crosswords and mystery novels came from him. I blossomed from his attention and developed a serious crush. He was the father I longed for - fair, kind, engaged, but never inappropriate in his attentions to me. With him I felt safe and accepted. But for Frances, it was a tricky situation. She was pregnant and as she told me later, feeling large and unattractive and a little threatened by this young woman she had brought into the family. Even her sisters and sister-in-law had thought it was risky and I did nothing to ease her mind. While not outright flirting with my new father, I certainly did things that made her feel doubly insecure. Once, I discovered that he had buttons missing from his pajama jacket and lovingly sewed them back on. He thanked her and she had to admit she hadn't done the sewing. I suspect that by my actions I had not only wanted to please my father, but also show my mother that she was not a sufficiently attentive wife.

And the fact that we were clashing over rules did not help. While Daddy accepted me as I was, Yorkshire accent and all, Mummy felt it was her to job to make me fit into her class-conscious model. I was not to say serviette but napkin, not toilet but lavatory. Shades of Mrs. Whitaker! I argued vehemently that the words I used were common in many languages and thus made sense. I was also chided for sending a postcard that began with a salutation instead of just starting with the message – apparently a social error that would mark me as an ignoramus. I argued that if people judged me on such matters, then they weren't worth bothering with. Mummy's reply was that if I wanted to be a Christopherson, I should accept her rules.

I was deeply disturbed by what I thought was a cruel comment. All my life I had strained to fit in with what different people wanted and now that I was showing a healthy re-examination of everything I had been taught, sorting out the things that made sense and rejecting others that sounded silly, I was being told that there was a price for joining the family. Immature as I was at that age, I did not understand nuance. I needed things to be either right or wrong and I challenged my mother on her rules or statements because I wanted to understand and evaluate the logic behind them.

For example, she warned me against drinking whiskey. Short drinks as they were called, made people drunk much quicker than beer or wine she counseled. When I asked her why, then, did she and Daddy often drink gin and tonics, she grew defensive and simply said that whiskey was a dreadful drink. It made no sense. In fact, I had once tried whiskey and found its taste medicinal, but I still wanted to pursue the logic of her argument. Much later, I learned that a close friend of hers had committed suicide after drinking a lot of whiskey and so she associated forever that loss with the drink. Had she told me that at the time, I would have certainly understood and sympathized with her point of view.

Both my parents were avid readers and belonged to a monthly book club. One of their books that caught my eye was a series of essays co-authored by Nancy Mitford, a satirical novelist. The book, *Noblesse Oblige: An Inquiry into the Identifiable Characteristics of the English Aristocracy,* was immensely popular. In it she divided the population into upper class (U's) and their opposites (Non-U's) depending on the choice of behavior they used. It was accompanied with drawings and my parents thought it hilarious. I did not understand at first that it was a parody of the class system in Britain, mocking people who looked down on others. In a strange way I found it funny, too, but also unpleasant because it touched a raw nerve. I don't think such a book would have been written in any other country but mine.

On the other hand, my parents gave me for Christmas a copy of Noel Streatfield's *"Growing Up Gracefully"* which was a thoughtful guide for instructing teenagers on good manners. Each chapter was written by a different author and had such wonderful titles as "How Eccentric May I Be?", "When Not To Make A Fuss", and "Don't Drop That Brick" and was introduced wittily by Streatfield and the drawings are wonderful. I loved the book and even though today it would seem adorably quaint, it nevertheless offered a great deal of wisdom that would be useful even today in this anything goes world we live in.

And of course, my mother's behavior contrasted sharply with Daddy's unconditional acceptance of me. Years later I was able to reconcile Mummy's extreme kindness towards those less fortunate, including me, with her strange emphasis on "proper" etiquette. She had been brought up in a very strict household with a domineering father, a lay preacher who would call her into his study to discuss the state of her soul, and a snobbish mother who was obsessed with social status. Her father's behavior chased her away from religion for a long time, but her mother's influence clung to her in spite of the fact that I think she was really an artistic soul yearning to be free to express herself. A classic picture of her comes to mind. She was entertaining friends for dinner and when we were enjoying coffee in the drawing room, she kicked off her shoes as she often did because her bunions were painful and sank thankfully down to the floor where she was always most comfortable. At some point, she realized what she had done and made an ungainly scramble to her feet and back into her chair. I think her guests who were close friends would have found her sitting on the floor quite charming, but the ensuing correction made the situation embarrassing. No wonder she loved America, which she visited often. She said she could be herself there and did not feel she had to be guarded in what she said.

I think her insistence on certain rules was in her mind part of her duty to give me the tools to navigate society, but her insecurities drove her to lay a bit of a heavy hand on me. For example, it bothered her immensely when she discovered years later that I had been working for an engineer who was at school with her husband. She insisted that I tell him I was adopted as she was nervous that he would work out that I had been born before she and Daddy were married.

Years later, when Daddy became Vice Chancellor of Durham University, her anxiety at keeping up socially became somewhat extreme and resulted in a fight with me as to what boarding school Peter should be sent to. I did not want him to go to boarding school at all, but Mummy was afraid that he would suffer from being brought up basically as an only child as we were all so much older than him, and she was reluctant to invite children to the house to play with Peter in case people thought she was playing favorites. Her choice of boarding school - a posh institution similar to my father's school that emphasized toughness through long cross country runs and cold showers and which my father loathed – was in my opinion totally wrong for Peter, who had no athletic interests and was already showing strong signs of following in her artistic footstep. Eventually, good sense prevailed and Peter ended up at a Quaker boarding school in Yorkshire that emphasized developing the individual interests of the pupils as well as being strong academically, and he flourished, developing his love of photography for which he became famous in later years. So we were all happy.

But these clashes in my first year and later were very different from those with the Whitakers. They did not upset my happiness or sense of stability. In fact, in a way they strengthened it. I sensed somehow for the first time that this was all normal family dynamics: I was behaving like a typical teenager, and they were behaving like typical parents. "Typical" had been an unknown but longed-for strand in my relationships. My mother's response to a confrontation with me with which I began this story gave me the freedom to test my independence of thought whether it was right or wrong without fearing a backlash.

In spite of the arguments, there were many tender moments between my mother and me and in fact I loved her every bit as much as I did Daddy. I recall one day, we were on the way home from a picnic when I commented that it was getting darker. "No", said Oliver, "it's just less light". I told Oliver I thought the statements meant the same but he went into a convoluted explanation of why that was not so. I rolled my eyes and Mummy said,

"Oh Annie, that's why I needed a daughter!" Ranged against three logical males, she had longed for someone who knew that sometimes feelings outweighed logic!

All communications to be addressed to the Children's Officer

CITY OF LEEDS
CARE OF CHILDREN DEPARTMENT

CYRIL PURNELL, B.A.,
CHILDREN'S OFFICER
TELEPHONE 31887-8-9

229, WOODHOUSE LANE,
LEEDS 2

Your Ref.

Our Ref. CP/AB

31st August, 1955.

Professor D.G. Christopherson,
43 Grove Lane,
Headingley,
LEEDS, 6.

Dear Professor Christopherson,

Many thanks for your letter regarding Ann. I am very pleased indeed to know that her marks throughout her examinations are satisfactory and you can rest assured that I feel equally proud of Ann and I extend to her every good wish for her future. In doing this I do not overlook all the help and guidance, care and affection that you and Mrs. Christopherson have extended to Ann, because now I really believe that she has found the niche which provides for her the feeling of security and affection for which she has been looking for many years.

I have been particularly interested in Ann's welfare and from time to time discussed her progress with Miss Baker. If at any time whilst you are resident in London any problem arises with which you feel I can be of assistance, do not hesitate to contact me. One thing I would make clear at the outset is that whilst young people normally leave the care of my Authority at the age of 18, it will be possible to extend maintenance and clothing payments in relation to Ann beyond this date and this I am sure my Committee will do without hesitation.

Regarding your comment about the arrangements for the allowance payments to be made to your wife when you take up residence at Wimbledon, any arrange-ments which you wish to make in this respect can be made with the Supervising Officer of the London County Council when she calls to see you or your wife and I am sure you will find her to be as co-operative and helpful as Miss Baker has been.

May I say that I hope you and the family will find your change to London to be a happy one and I would also like, once again, to say how much I do appreciate all that you are doing on behalf of Ann, because I do feel that the prospects for Ann are quite rosy and that she will continue to make excellent progress.

I see that Ann has decided to use the name "Christopherson" and this is perhaps a natural decision on her part but she should, of course, over a period, adjust herself to the explanations that may be necessary from time to time in the course of her career.

Yours sincerely,

Children's Officer.

The official response to the Christopherson's request for me to live with them in London

All communications to be addressed to the Children's Officer

CITY OF LEEDS

CARE OF CHILDREN DEPARTMENT

CYRIL PURNELL, B.A.,
CHILDREN'S OFFICER
TELEPHONE: 31957-8-9

229, WOODHOUSE LANE,
LEEDS 2

Your Ref.....................

Our Ref.....................   CP/BAL

11th December, 1959.

D. C. Christopherson, Esq.,
9 Burghley Road,
Wimbledon,
LONDON, S.W.19.

Dear Professor Christopherson,

I have, to-day's date, received a letter from my colleague informing me that your application, on yesterday's date, to adopt Ann, was successful.

There is little that I can add to previous correspondence except to say that I do feel that you have filled a large place in Ann's heart. For many years, she has been searching anxiously for the care and affection which you have so readily extended to her. That she will take great pride in, and obtain joy from the adoption, is not doubted, and the purpose of my brief note is to say how my Committee appreciate all you have done on behalf of Ann.

On their behalf, I extend to you their expressions of appreciation and would add how personally, I am happy that the adoption has materialised. To you both, I would not only say thank you, but would extend to you every good wish for the future and sincerely hope that the present happy relationship in relation to Ann, long continues.

Yours sincerely,

Children's Officer.

The official approval of my adoption

Peter's christening at St. Chad's,
Headingly, 1955.

Winning the 100 yard dash, Sports Day, 1955

Receiving the overall sports   Class hike in theYorkshire Dales,
award, 1955   1955

Scotland, with Rosalind and her brother Roland, 1955

Chapter 6: 9, Burghley Road, Wimbledon
1955

In late summer, we headed off to our new home in London. My parents had chosen the suburb of Wimbledon in south-west London because it was close to Raines Park where Aunt Mary lived and they wanted to help with the care of her senile mother, and because there were good schools for James and me. The house was a three story structure in a pretty street close to the All England Lawn Tennis Association and a short walk to Wimbledon Village, a group of elegant shops and the Dog and Fox Inn all clustered at the top of a steep hill.

A stone's throw away was Wimbledon Common, and if you were strenuous enough to walk over it and cross the busy Kingston Bypass, you ended up in beautiful Richmond Park. At the bottom of the hill was my new school, Wimbledon School for Girls, more shops, the library, post office, and the railway station serving both the Green Line of the Underground and the Southern Railway which terminated at Waterloo Station. The houses in and around the Village were owned for the most part by affluent people, many of whom had French au pair girls to help with the children.

The area below the station was less attractive but it did have one important establishment – a fish and chip shop. The inhabitants of the Village had fought strongly to deny a fish and chip shop at the top of the hill, citing litter from newspapers as their main objection. So, when we wanted to have fish and chips for dinner, Daddy and I took the bus down the hill to buy them. In those days, fish and chips were first wrapped in greaseproof paper and then in lots of newspaper to keep them warm until you got home. It was common to take newspapers to the shop to contribute to the supply and also a good way of getting rid of them. Daddy and I would then take the bus back, savoring the wonderful smells coming from the still warm package while occasionally grinning at the disapproving sniffs of some of our fellow passengers. My father joked that thanks to the au pair girls, we were probably the only people who had their fish and chips wrapped in *Le Figaro*!

My father also stirred in me an interest in politics and the only time I saw him truly angry was during the Suez crisis. He was furious at the secret collusion between France, Britain and Israel to attack Egypt for nationalizing the Suez Canal. He and I went to Trafalgar Square to take part in a huge anti-government rally. During a quiet moment between speakers, my mild-mannered father, to my astonishment, yelled at the top of his lungs, "Eden Must Go", referring to the Prime Minister Sir Anthony Eden. The crowd took up the chant and I was torn between embarrassment and pride at what he had started. But then the crowd became unruly as its leaders started off down Whitehall towards 10, Downing Street, the official residence of the Prime Minister, and some of them threw marbles under the police horses, a common tactic by protesters to make the horses skid and unseat the officers. I was horrified at this turn of events, as was my father, and he quickly grabbed me by the hand and hurried me away from the mob to the nearest Underground station. Amazingly, I learned many years later that my future American husband attended that demonstration, too!

In the autumn term, I entered Wimbledon High School, which was situated at the bottom of Wimbledon Hill. James went to King's College School, an independent day school with a fine academic record and Oliver continued at Worcester College for the Blind. Always acutely conscious of being a financial burden, I was very concerned that my parents would have to pay fees but was reassured when they told me that the County of Surrey where we now lived had agreed to continue the foster care support begun in Yorkshire.

Wimbledon High School was smaller than my Leeds school but had a similar emphasis on educating its girls to be well rounded citizens. In its brochure, it lists the following School Course: Religious Knowledge, Reading, Writing, Mathematics, English Grammar, Composition and Literature, History, Geography, French, German, Latin, Greek, Chemistry, Physics, Biology, Art, Class Singing, Musical Appreciation and Harmony, Handiwork and Needlework, Gymnastics, Dancing and Games. Sports were not much emphasized and I can only remember hockey being played. I became a member of the first team and we practiced and played on what was once the site of the All England Lawn Tennis Association until it moved to its present location.

The Head Mistress, Miss Burke, was much more approachable than Miss Sykes and much more down to earth. Based on a photograph in her flat, it was rumored that she had been romantically involved with Rupert Brooke, the dashing English poet who wrote idealistic poems about war, but since he died in 1915, I think that would not be likely.

I entered the sixth form to spend two years preparing for A Level, the exams that would, if I did well in them, gain me a place at a university. The curriculum in English grammar schools was very different from that of American schools. The subjects you chose to study (usually only three or four at most) in the sixth form articulated closely with the subjects you would specialize in at university, and you had to decide on those subjects early on in your school life in order to enter the right stream of either arts or science. Once those early decisions had been made, it was extremely hard to reverse them. I knew of only one girl who did this. She had chosen science subjects, in her case due to pressure from her parents who were both doctors, and then later switched to arts and ultimately excelled brilliantly at history and became a member of the British government.

Because of this system of early specialization, you did not apply for a place at a university but rather to a department at that university. The narrow choices we were forced to make at an early age meant that you tended to choose the subjects you were good at without knowing anything about other areas that might be of interest to you in later life. Because I was good at languages, I chose French, German and English, but Wimbledon School told me that if I wanted to try to win a place at the prestigious universities of Oxford or Cambridge, I would have to include Latin. (The number of students who won such places had their names inscribed on plaques and added greatly to the prestige of the school.) I had done reasonably well at Latin at O Level because that had required mostly understanding the grammar and learning the vocabulary, but struggled greatly when the advanced studies included reading in the original the great works of Latin literature.

I was readily accepted into the school by my fellow pupils and my Yorkshire accent began to disappear. But although I participated in some school events, playing a minor role in a Shakespeare play, and being on the hockey team, for example, I never felt the same strong attachment that I did to my Leeds school and I missed Rosalind. The memory, however, of one glorious occasion at this school has stayed with me forever. Our very enterprising music teacher decided the whole school would learn the choral parts of Hayden's great work *The Creation.* It was an ambitious project and at first we balked at all the rehearsals but eventually as the work unfolded, we began to be excited. The soloists came from outside and professional musicians that the teacher knew supplemented the school orchestra. The parents were invited and we sang our hearts out. I can still remember the shiver that went through me as I sang the words "Let there be Light".

Christmas with the family was a very joyous occasion, full of traditions which my mother delighted in. When we departed for bed, we hung one of her nylon stockings on the bedpost which sometime in the night she exchanged for a duplicate stocking filled with traditional gifts: an orange or tangerine in the toe, a bag of chocolate coins and other sweets and a special gift. Major presents were placed under the tree to be opened after breakfast. As we got older, Peter was the only one to receive a stocking and since he was determined to stay awake long enough to catch Father Christmas in the act, my tired mother, who had been working all day getting food ready for Christmas Day and who wanted badly to sleep in a bit the next morning before starting the task of cooking the turkey, the Christmas pudding, and other traditional foods, had to stay up very late before she could sneak in and make the stocking exchange. Once, to many giggles, she dressed up as Father Christmas in case Peter wasn't fully asleep.

To let her sleep in, I agreed that Peter should come into my bed with his stocking, but not before 5 o'clock, and we exclaimed with pleasure as he pulled out the gifts. It was a treasured ritual and I looked forward to it every year. Inevitably, Peter questioned the logistics of Father Christmas flying around the world and climbing down chimneys and confessed he had stopped believing quite some time ago but didn't admit to it because he wanted to see who it was who came into his room.

We hung mistletoe in strategic places and decorated the house with the inevitable paper chains, as well as a beautiful tree. Mummy carefully placed real candles on the safest branches and on Christmas Day my father lit them and turned out the lights so we could appreciate this magical moment. My mother stood by with a bucket of water in case the tree, now draped in lots of tinsel, should catch fire. Christmas Dinner was timed to finish at 3 o'clock so we could listen to the Queen's Speech on the radio. We ate turkey which my father carved ceremoniously at the table, sage and onion stuffing, mashed potatoes and gravy and vegetables, and then Christmas pudding which was soaked in brandy and brought to the table in flames. My mother hid shiny new sixpences in the pudding and later lucky charms. On the table were beautiful Christmas crackers which we pulled in unison, crossing our arms over our chests to get the maximum force. The crackers contained very corny jokes which we read out to much groaning, silly trinkets, and a paper hat which we immediately put on. I hated destroying the crackers because they were so beautifully decorated. At around 5:30, with our stomachs still full, my mother made cups of tea and brought in slices of traditional Christmas cake – a rich fruit caked topped with marzipan and hard imperial icing.

During my first year at Wimbledon High School, my parents agreed to let me take part in a huge exchange involving French and British grammar school pupils. We were to spend three weeks in Paris during the Easter holidays at the home of a French family, and in turn, our hosts would spend three weeks in England during the summer. A huge contingent of excited young people descended on Victoria Station to board the train to Dover, then on the ferry to Calais, and finally another train to Paris, where we were met by the host families.

It must have been quite a logistical challenge for the organizers, but somehow we all ended up with the right families. I was matched with a girl called Catherine, a tall, well-built young woman with the stunning combination of glossy black curls, blue eyes and a deep tan. Her younger sister, who had the more typical French petite figure, was matched with a girl from the upper fifth in my school. We discovered that the family lived in a flat in the sixteenth arrondissement of Paris, which I later learned was a very posh address, and so we climbed into a taxi to be driven to their home. I was busy taking in all the sounds and sights of Paris, and was startled when our taxi came to a sudden, jarring halt. Two drivers who had collided in the heavy traffic had abandoned their vehicles and were engaged in a heated argument, causing a massive traffic jam.

While our taxi driver was drumming his fingers on the steering wheel in frustration and uttering oaths under his breath, others had climbed out of their cars, hoping to see a fight. I thought if that had happened in London, bobbies would have arrived and sorted it all out quite calmly, whereas the gendarmes, when they eventually turned up, seemed to be running around blowing their whistles, contributing to the chaos. I thoroughly enjoyed the whole spectacle and hoped I would experience more examples of Gallic temperament. Eventually we arrived and I discovered a family so very different from my own.

Catherine's mother was a widow. Although not really pretty, she was petite, slender, extremely elegant, and had died blonde hair – something I had never seen before on a woman of her class. She lived a life of luxury with a maid to take care of her every need. She never got up much before noon, and after a light breakfast of café au lait and a croissant would spend the next hour in her bath into which her maid poured from a huge bottle some French perfume called Ma Griffe. It was at the time my favorite perfume and I treasured the tiny bottle I had purchased at great cost in London, using it sparingly for special occasions. I goggled at the enormous bottle and couldn't imagine wasting it in the bathwater.

After lunch, her mother would invite her friends to play bridge and in the evenings she mysteriously disappeared. She seemed fond of her two daughters but did not engage much with them, shipping them off to ski in the Christmas holidays (hence the deep tan) and to the family seaside home at Les Sables D'Orlonne in the spring and summer. Catherine and her sister took us to the more famous Parisian sights and then the mystery of where her mother disappeared to every evening was resolved when an elegant limousine turned up to take us on a tour of Paris by night. Apparently, this lady was the mayor's mistress and to please her he had arranged this little trip for us.

It was a magical tour for us and very amusing as in spite of the signs everywhere forbidding people to sound their horns, the Mayor's official car blared its way around all the sights. We ended up at City Hall and the charming Mayor signed for each of us a book by Robert Doisneau, *"Les Parisiens Tels Qu'ils Sont"* (roughly translated, What Parisians are Like.)

For the last week we were dispatched to the seaside, and the other English girl and I were subjected to the close scrutiny of Catherine's many relatives and friends. They admired my English skin but debated in front of me whether it was truly flawless or whether I used concealing face powder. It was very disconcerting. I felt like the little girl in Hansel and Gretel and wondered if next they would start poking me like the witch.

Catherine and I were tolerant of each other but wedded not really hit it off and I suspect we both wondered how we would survive another three weeks together in the summer. My family life, of course, was the exact opposite of hers. I think she may have enjoyed to some extent the warm family life we had and the presence of my younger brothers, but she grumbled a great deal, especially when my parents took her with us to see the sights in Cambridge. Instead of enjoying the stroll around the beautiful colleges, she bemoaned the fact that she had to walk so much.

"Mes pieds, mes pieds" (my feet, my feet) she kept saying, and so it amused us greatly when after her visit, her thank-you letter included the statement that the highlight of her visit had been the trip to Cambridge!

A great change for me was that at sixteen years of age I finally experienced for the first time a social life – a big first step in learning how to interact with my peers, especially boys, outside the classroom. I joined the youth club of St. Mary's, the nearby church that the family sporadically attended, and took part in a lot of wholesome activities such as hiking, and putting on plays and dances. At Christmas we pushed around a small organ which a young man could play and we went door to door singing carols.

We finished up at the vicarage where we were invited to sing and then given delicious hot mince pies. One of the most amusing episodes was getting up in the middle of the night during the final weekend of the Wimbledon tennis tournament and serving snacks to the people queuing up all night for tickets to the Men's Final the next day. The money we earned went into the Youth Club coffers.

The tennis tournament was a very big event for the people of Wimbledon. The Australian players were the best in the world at that time and were rock stars to the girls at Wimbledon High School. Aunt Mary played tennis and was a big fan too. After the death of her mother, she had moved to a charming cottage just off the High Street and opened her home every year to two umpires. She gave them breakfast before the start of play in the morning, and a cup of tea and biscuits in the evening and then listened to them as they discussed the day's play and sometimes juicy details about the players which she passed on to me. Even better, the man who delivered milk to the Tennis Association was given two weeks of tickets to the tournament for his Christmas tip and not caring for tennis, exchanged them with my mother for two hundred cigarettes.

Every day during the fortnight he would leave two tickets under the milk bottles and I would rush home from school at 3:30 to claim one. I changed out of my school uniform and put on my grown-up clothes and teetered down to the courts on my high heels. The tickets were for entrance to the grounds and the outer courts only, but my goal was Center Court, where the best matches were played. I stationed myself at one of the exits.

Tennis started at 2 o'clock and the first match would be over soon after I arrived. Right on time, people began to pour out of the court and I would zero in like a laser on any man who looked like a company executive. With a sweet smile, I would ask him if he planned on using his ticket anymore that day and almost always he was heading home and happily gave up the ticket. So, every day from 4 o'clock until 9 when it got too dark for play, I watched some great tennis stars play some riveting matches: Billy Jean King, Althea Gibson (first African American woman at Wimbledon), Margaret Court, Roy Emerson, Rod Laver, and a special favorite of mine, Yvonne Goolagong. I was agog at a deeply tanned glamorous California woman, Carol Fagaros, who was a lingerie model when not playing tennis and looked stunning in a dress that looked like a Greek toga, and indignant at Australian Lew Hoad who got his girlfriend pregnant and had a hasty marriage at my church.

This was the time of strictly amateur play and there was no prize money offered for the players. The low-level players who usually got knocked out in the early rounds could not afford to stay at a hotel so the locals offered them free accommodation. It was customary for the players to attend a ball after the tournament and the first dance was performed by the two champions.

Some of my friends, whose mothers had hosted a player, were invited to go to the dance. I begged my mother to offer our top floor to a player but alas she refused. Now, tickets from people leaving the courts early are turned into a special box and resold for charity and the lines for those are almost as long as the lines to get into the grounds.

Tennis was not the only source of teen fervor. When I was seventeen, Bill Hailey and the Comets released their first rock 'n roll record, *Rock Around the Clock* and we were all crazy about this music. We reacted to the loud, strong beat just begging you to get up and dance. Music in the 40's had been to a large extent pretty sophisticated in its lyrics and orchestration and had found favor with everyone, but rock 'n roll was music that appealed directly to teens because many of the bands were teenagers themselves, and the lyrics, however simplistic, spoke to teenage angst.

Some adults condemned the music and its singers, especially Elvis Presley, whose sensual good looks and wiggling hips they felt sure would lead us to perdition, but that only made the music more appealing. When he appeared on television on the Ed Sullivan Show in America, he was only filmed from the waist up so as not to give offense.

At age seventeen, I developed my first attachment to a young man. Alan Jones, a member of my youth club, lived with his mother in Wimbledon Village. He was gentle, kind and funny. He sang in the church choir and I later learned that he had been one of the choristers at the Queen's coronation. He had soulful deep brown eyes. I started attending evensong more often, sitting upstairs in the balcony, and looking forhim as he frequently turned those bewitching eyes on me. We parted when I went off to University and he headed to a New York seminary to train for the clergy. Later, he became the Dean of Grace Cathedral in San Francisco.

I gave up on the idea of Oxford or Cambridge. I was clearly not bright or confident enough to be accepted into those prestigious institutions, and to be honest, I was not comfortable with their culture. I met a student from Cambridge who told me that one of her favorite things to do with her friends was having Pooh parties, i.e., sitting around a room reading Winnie the Pooh stories and eating honey, and I shuddered at the thought of trying to fit in with the kind of people who thought such activity fun. Of course, that was not representative of everybody at those elite institutions. Rosalind found her way and did very well. So, I applied instead to the French Department at the University of Bristol.

The department had a good reputation for French and I wanted to explore a different part of England. They accepted me provisionally, dependent on receiving certain marks in A Level, which I managed to accomplish. Thank goodness they only required a pass in Latin! Much to my joy, the local authorities continued to support me financially through my three years at Bristol even though I had passed the age of eighteen when such support would normally end. In Britain in those days, only five percent of young people went to university, which were strictly academic, although there were many other higher education possibilities such as schools of nursing, architecture and art, and polytechnics. I think I was possibly the first child in carefrom Yorkshire to go to a university so the authorities were anxious to continue to support me.

So at age eighteen I went off to Bristol, but there was one more issue to be resolved before I finally felt fully grounded and safe. My parents had earlier wanted to officially adopt me but I felt secure enough to tell them I could wait as I did not want them to have to pay for higher education, and this decision of mine was a reflection of my total trust in them.

In December of my third and final year at Bristol, my mother rang me to say that it had suddenly occurred to them that they had to adopt me before I turned twenty-one, the age of majority at that time. My birthday was late January and even though it would mean they had to pay for the summer term, I joyfully agreed. Later, she called back and asked if I would like to add or change my Christian name. My roommates, Jill, Julie, and Cappy, sat on the floor with me while we came up with ridiculous combinations of names.

The proceedings took place on the 10th of December, 1959, in the Kingston upon Thames County Court. It sadly was an unpleasant occasion. The judge could not understand why I was being adopted at such a late age and accused me of being after my parents' money, which was ironic since I had delayed adoption precisely to save them the cost of my university education.

With much grumbling, he approved the adoption and I became Frances Ann Christopherson!

In the back garden in
Wimbledon, 1957

Wimbledon, 1957

On holiday at Treyarnon Bay, Cornwall, 1957

Peter already a budding
photographer, 1957

With Alan Jones in *The
Importance of Being Earnest, 1957*

Application photograph for Bristol University, 1957

Christopherson family in Cambridge, 1984

Back row: left to right: Peter, Audrey, Oliver, Robin, James, Robert,
Pippa Jo, Richard
Middle row: Kari Anna, my parents, me and Sarah.
Front row: Stephanie, Simon and Matthew.

Postscript

Many of you will wonder what happened to me and my four siblings. Here is what I know today:

Norma, the youngest married twice and had three children. She eventually moved to Bournemouth on the south coast of England. She is very active in the Salvation Army. Sadly, I have yet to meet her.

John was adopted by his foster family and is happily married with one daughter and two grandchildren. He was a plumber for many years and then became a Senior Maintenance Surveyor for the Department of Housing and Environmental Health.

John Spurr and my brother John
at my Sister Mary's wedding

Mary (Doris) met her husband, John, at 18 when she worked in the Leeds Post Office Building, and has three children, six grandchildren, and five great grandchildren. John died many years ago of a heart attack.

Barry, who went to live with his father, ran away from home to escape brutal beatings and eventually joined the forces. He married, had two children and several grandchildren. He died recently.

Barry Spurr in the Army

As for **me**, I married Robert, an American professor of political science. He died in 2015 of cancer. I have twin children and 4 grandchildren.

Anna and Robert Berdahl

Made in the USA
Columbia, SC
30 November 2019